The Teaching for Social Justice Series

William Ayers—Series Editor
Therese Quinn—Associate Series Editor

Editorial Board: Hal Adams, Barbara Bowman, Lisa Delpit, Michelle Fine, Maxine Greene, Caroline Heller, Annette Henry, Asa Hilliard (1933–2007), Rashid Khalidi, Kevin Kumashiro, Gloria Ladson-Billings, Erica Meiners, Charles Payne, Luis Rodriguez, Jonathan Silin, William Watkins

Controversies in the Classroom

A *RADICAL TEACHER* READER

EDITED BY
Joseph Entin
Robert C. Rosen
Leonard Vogt

Foreword by Deborah Meier

Teachers College, Columbia University
New York and London

Published by Teachers College Press, 1234 Amsterdam Avenue, New York, NY 10027

Library of Congress Cataloging-in-Publication Data

Controversies in the classroom : a radical teacher reader / edited by Jospeh Entin, Robert C. Rosen, and Leonard Vogt ; foreword by Deborah Meier.
     p.   cm. — (The teaching for social justice series)
  Includes bibliographical references and index.
  ISBN 978-0-8077-4911-1 (pbk : alk. paper) — ISBN 978-0-8077-4912-8 (cloth : alk. paper)
    1. Critical pedagogy—United States.   2. Social justice—Study and teaching—United States. I. Entin, Joseph B. II. Rosen, Robert C., 1947– III. Vogt, Leonard, 1943–

  LC196.5.U6C68 2008
  370.11'5—dc22

                                     2008018735

ISBN 978-0-8077-4911-1 (paper)
ISBN 978-0-8077-4912-8 (cloth)

Printed on acid-free paper
Manufactured in the United States of America

15 14 13 12 11 10 09 08   8 7 6 5 4 3 2 1

In memory of Harald Bakken, Constance Coiner,
Shafali Lal, and Liz Powell

Contents

Series Foreword

GOODBYE TO teaching that is smug and self-satisfied, teaching as authoritative and proud, hiding its conflicts and uncertainties behind a lectern, a textbook, or a "social science" conceit. Goodbye to teaching as clerking—something quickly learned, easily assessed, instantly remediated. Goodbye to teaching as a trivial pursuit of the obvious.

Welcome to an approach that is overflowing with life, crackling with the surprising and contradictory harmonies of intimacy and love, stunning in its hope for a better world. Welcome to teaching as value-laden, aspirational, and imperfect—a never-ending voyage of discovery and surprise, a continuous work-in-progress. Welcome to a life of no easy answers.

Because we want to live in a fully human world, a world of mutual recognition, we want to develop a richer and deeper vision of justice, and a pedagogy of justice as well, something that tries to see the world as it is, and tries to stand against violence and war and exploitation and oppression, tries to act for love and fairness and balance and peace—a pedagogy that begins to enact the power of love that does justice.

Teaching for social justice resists the metaphor of teaching as a simple stimulus-response binary: teacher speaks and acts, student receives and takes in. It resists the notion that good teaching can be reduced to an isolated variable, and then measured on some simple-minded standardized scale. Teaching for social justice resists the increasing militarization of schools, the privatization of public education, and the hollowing out of curriculum to serve a reduced sense of education as nothing more than job training.

Teaching for social justice begins and ends with questions—for ourselves, for our students: What's my story? How did I get here? How is my story like or unlike other stories? What are we going to do? What do I want? What are my chances? We embrace a curriculum of questions and a practice of doing and making.

Social justice teaching tries to tell the truth. We want to experience, imagine, and create, and we want to seek all evidence and report fully and honestly. Social justice teachers make expansive maps of possibility with students. We listen and bear witness to unnecessary suffering and pain. We open spaces for rethinking and reinventing ourselves and our world.

Goodbye to being in control all the time. Goodbye to overthinking and underexperiencing. Goodbye to deference, didacticism, ego, and the need to always be right. Goodbye to complacency in a heartless world. Goodbye to prisons and border guards and walls—whether in Palestine or in Texas or inside our own classrooms or our own hearts and minds. Goodbye to all that.

Welcome to the unknown, to jumping off the edge, to the new and the now, to endlessly learning how to live again and how to love anew. Welcome to relentless curiosity, simple acts of kindness, the complexity of humanity, the wonder of it all. Embrace struggle and world peace and inner peace; embrace all kinds of love for all kinds of people in all kinds of circumstances and situations. Embrace teaching with one foot in the hard reality of the here and the now, and another striding toward a world that could be but is not yet.

Foreword

THERE ARE DAYS when it just makes no sense that we "incarcerate" the young for 12 or more years inside the four walls of a school building. Of course, that's a harsh and provocative description, but technically correct. They have committed no crime, but it's a crime for them not to go to school. For 5 or 6 hours a day, their freedom is severely restricted. Whether their parents like it or not, that's where they must be.

Still, I'm not against mandatory schooling. It was a progressive achievement, and I am not proposing that we eliminate it. But unless we take seriously the implications of our actions, we cannot wisely understand how schooling plays out in reality.

We don't need fancy language for telling us a simple, age-old truth: The task of learning must be the work of the learner. It's in the nature of being human that we learn—although not necessarily what teachers and society intend for us to learn. Children, from birth on, know how to learn, and are even remarkably efficient and productive at doing so. It's unstoppable.

But adults, including even the radical teachers whose writing appears in this collection, have their agendas about what learning is to take place in our schools, with consequences that have an enormous impact on their "imprisoned" students. The dilemma for all of us—traditional and radical alike—is how to enlist the voluntary energies of those required to spend their time in our schools on behalf of our particular definition of the cause. Sometimes our causes are more attractive to some or most kids, and sometimes less so. Sometimes our pedagogy is more or less engaging. But even our best ideals often confront hostility, refusal, or just boredom. We cajole or threaten, and squeeze a little of the intended learning into the young. It drifts in and out pretty fast. We are frustrated, and we up the ante—more dire penalties for failure to learn, more bonuses for success.

The most excitement, of an intellectual sort, that I experienced while working at my last school, Mission Hill, occurred when an 11-year-old boy tried to explain to me and his classmates that we were doomed to hell—and that this was not just his opinion, but the truth. He was sincere. More important, he was smart and thoughtful in his argument, and it attracted a substantial crowd. Even had I wanted to, I doubt if I could have put a stop to it. Instead, we all moved into an empty classroom (it was the beginning of lunchtime), and the spontaneous conversation went on and on. Everyone had another point to make. After it finally ended (influenced by a desire for food), I nervously dashed into the office to send a letter to the families of the students involved. I explained how proud I was of their ability to engage in a wonderful and courteous—and heated—discussion, and that I hoped they'd continue it at home. I was covering myself, in case it came home in a distorted version. But I also meant it.

Kids love a good argument; they have serious questions about the world. Their questions are sometimes factual, but often philosophical.

And too often, we dread their questions—in part, of course, because our responses may be badly misunderstood, but also because they may be too well understood. In both cases, their questions and our responses may produce a furor. Time constraints alone often dictate that we avoid controversy. Yet at the heart of being a "good citizen of a democracy" is learning how to develop well-grounded views, and then dealing with the controversy surrounding them. We'd hardly need democracy if everyone always agreed. The habits of mind (and heart) that schools "teach" are precisely those that help us deal with disagreement and doubt. We should therefore be constantly alert for opportunities to create both.

How do human beings go about discovering truth? is our underlying question. How do we uncover the varied viewpoints that exist beside our own? How do we sift through them, looking for patterns, past examples, possible consequences? What kind of evidence serves what kind of problem well? Does it matter or not, and to whom?

Twelve years of schooling surely have an impact. They teach lessons. But what they too often teach is how to avoid having an opinion at all—or at least how to avoid making it public. They teach too many how to figure out what the authorities want them to say, believe, answer. There's no place in a multiple choice test for maybes, or explanations. The good students get very adept at reading the cues scattered all about them. The others don't get it, or refuse to attend to it, or turn their back on it all. They learn strategies for evading, sabotaging, and disrupting—sometimes out of opposition, sometimes to protect their egos, sometimes out of boredom. What a waste of everyone's time, we say.

The radical teachers who tell their stories and present their ideas in this collection are looking at ways to build classrooms and schools that excite kids, that join them in their queries about the world, that present the world as a fascinating mystery that needs to be solved if they are to enter it with their own voices. We are hoping to engage the young in inquiries that they didn't ever imagine might interest them, and leave them wanting more.

It's hard work, and what works for one teacher doesn't always work for another. Sometimes it's a matter of sheer charisma, but most often it's a question of hard-won respect and trust—the steady work of teaching day in, day out. It comes more easily in schools in which the faculty is a community of learners, when families and community assume their beliefs are respected, and when we thus dare to open the Pandora's box that lies before us in this collection.

—Deborah Meier

Acknowledgments

THIS BOOK would not have been possible without the efforts of the many members of the *Radical Teacher* editorial board. David Peck and Penny Dugan were especially helpful in the early stages of this project, and Shana Agid towards the end. We would also like to thank the people at Teachers College Press who worked with us: Judy Berman, Lyn Grossman, Golnar Nikpour, and Carole Saltz.

Introduction

PROGRESSIVE EDUCATORS have long had a significant impact on educational practice and policy across the United States. Inspired by the social justice movements of the 1960s and after—the civil rights, gay/lesbian, women's, and antiwar movements—left educators, including those of us associated with the journal *Radical Teacher*, have promoted teaching that is student centered and antiauthoritarian, self-reflexive and creative. We have aimed to encourage independence and initiative rather than treat students as empty vessels to be filled with knowledge delivered from on high, to expand teaching methods and curricular content to meet the varied needs of an increasingly diverse student population, and to encourage critical thinking that challenges official myths and seeks out the root causes of inequality and injustice. And our ideas have spread, as many of the approaches pioneered by teachers committed to social justice have been adopted in classrooms around the country.

Recently, however, a renewed and vigorous counterattack against progressive educational innovations has arisen. Conservatives (and others) have been promoting English-only education, an expanded role for the private sector in public education, and uniform standards for students and schools through one-size-fits-all testing and assessment. Their efforts, often financed by wealthy individuals, right-wing foundations, or large corporations, have included the English-only movement, which has sponsored ballot initiatives in several states; the advancement of private, for-profit companies, such as Edison Schools, Inc., to run public schools; and, perhaps most important in recent years, No Child Left Behind, the Bush administration–sponsored bill that was signed into federal law in 2001. NCLB was met with substantial criticism, and for good reason. The act's promotion of high-stakes testing to determine school success and punitive sanctions for schools judged to be failing promised to demoralize and constrain teachers and penalize rather than support struggling schools. As the dangers of NCLB have become more apparent (and the federal government's failure to fund it adequately more burdensome), opposition

1

has mounted; legislation rejecting all or part of NCLB has been introduced in every one of the fifty states.

The essays in this volume, published earlier in *Radical Teacher*, were written in this contradictory context—of a vibrant movement for progressive education confronted by an active and well-financed conservative commitment to reestablish traditional forms of schooling. And no less important, we think, is the even larger context for this domestic battle—the intensification of globalization and the new "war on terror." Together, these essays offer strategies for teaching against the grain in today's educational institutions, techniques for helping students to think critically about contemporary social and political issues, and moral and intellectual support for continuing to work in progressive ways in schools that are increasingly accountable to bottom-line, corporate-driven standards.

Radical Teacher itself originated in a particular social context, the social movements of the late 1960s and early 1970s. The Modern Language Association, the hidebound professional organization of college English and foreign-language teachers, was seized at that time with conflicts over the Vietnam War and other issues and, like many similar organizations, gave birth to a "Radical Caucus." By 1975, the caucus's newsletter had evolved into a journal—with an editorial board and a (somewhat) regular publishing schedule. The board soon expanded and became more diverse, as did its readership and stable of contributors, to include people from a wide variety of academic fields and, more important here, teachers at all levels. Our first collection, *The Politics of Education: Essays from "Radical Teacher"* (1990), reflects the journal's origins in higher education, but the present volume is devoted entirely to essays of interest and value to present and future teachers in schools.

Though the word *radical* these days can suggest anything from "terrorist" to "groovy," we believe the name *Radical Teacher* has served us and our readers well. For us, *radical* denotes a commitment to peace, justice, and progressive social change; the term is broad enough to encompass the variety of critical perspectives that our contributors have brought to the journal yet still underscores the importance of getting to the root of social and educational problems. And the word *teacher* keeps the emphasis on the practical activity—informed, to be sure, by serious theoretical thinking and debate—of the educational worker meeting students in the classroom.

This collection of 16 essays from *Radical Teacher* offers alternative curricula and teaching strategies to help counter the threats against political engagement, creativity, and hope that continue to confront both new and seasoned teachers. These essays are anchored in radical pedagogical theory and many of them offer detailed suggestions for putting progressive educational ideas into action, teaching strategies that you could read about on Sunday night and put into practice Monday morning. *Controversies in the Classroom* shares the experiences of elementary, middle, and high school teachers who have reflected, have taught, and have reconsidered their approaches in a wide variety of classroom situations.

We begin the collection with the section Teaching About War, for nothing today so challenges Americans and their consciences as our continuing occupation of Iraq in the name of fighting terrorism. Bill Bigelow's essay, "Whose Terrorism?", describes classroom activities that encourage students to work out their own definition of terrorism and then apply it to actual world events. The United States government has used the "war on terrorism" as a justification for a wide range of aggressive actions abroad and repressive actions at home, and Bigelow's curriculum invites students to broaden and refine their own ideas about terrorism and to test them against a variety of scenarios. H. Bruce Franklin's contribution, "Can Vietnam Awaken Us Again? Teaching the Literature of the Vietnam War," argues that today's students can best learn to critically examine and to challenge the official stories told about the Iraq war by looking, from a distance, at the lies told about the war in Vietnam. The literature of the Vietnam War, Franklin writes, can be a powerful "transformative force" in the thought and lives of students who study it. Finally in this section, Rita Verma's essay, "Dialogues About 9/11, the Media, and Race: Lessons from a Secondary Classroom," describes one way that the impact of war and terrorism can be felt in the classroom itself. Verma, a South Asian, was deeply affected by the racist aftermath of the events of 9/11, by the distorting media stereotypes and irrational hostilities, and through the sharing of her experiences with her students, she was able to open up an opportunity for the Arabs and South Asians among them to feel comfortable sharing their own stories.

Controversies in the Classroom continues with the section Teaching About Globalization. This economic, political, and cultural trend has recently become a major focus of debate, activism, and teaching. From the World Trade Organization protests in Seattle to antisweatshop campaigns, student activists have been demonstrating, if not against globalization, then in support of "global justice." Worldwide political and economic changes have often meant very personal changes for our students. Many of them have fled countries that suffer the effects of corporate globalization. Students face shaky funding for public education, increased high-stakes testing, and other strictures imposed by No Child Left Behind, for as global competition has intensified, education has become more corporatized—measured, rationed, privatized.

Arthur MacEwan's essay, "What Is Globalization?", provides a framework for understanding the history of this phenomenon, what is and isn't

new globally, and why globalization matters so much today. Globalization, he explains, has been around for centuries, but new trade agreements,
intensified international competition, and the increased power of the World
Trade Organization and similar institutions are what make the difference—
as does a large global response that includes labor, environmental,
women's, peasant, and student groups. In "Sweating the Small Stuff:
Mickey, Michael, and the Global Sweatshop," Maria Sweeney and Marjorie
Feld describe how an elementary school class spent weeks researching and
writing a play about global sweatshops only to have the school administration forbid them from performing it for the other students. Luckily, after
major news coverage embarrassing to the school, a New York director came
to their rescue and the play was performed on Broadway. In the following essay, fifth-grade teacher Bob Peterson tells his students about his living in Cairo as a teenager and being shocked when Egyptian children
desperately wanted the soda cans he was throwing away. In "Planting
Seeds of Solidarity" he describes how he moves from this story into a series
of lessons that help his students develop a feeling of solidarity with others
around the world—an important alternative to the "us"-versus-"them"
perspective that often seeps into global lessons.

Conflict and solidarity are of course enacted nationally and locally as
well as globally, and so we continue with a section, Teaching About Race,
Ethnicity, and Language. In "Revisiting the Struggle for Integration,"
Michelle Fine and Bernadette Anand describe a high school civil rights oral
history project in which Montclair, New Jersey, public school students
studied 25 years of local news reporting and uncovered for themselves the
history of segregation and media bias in their town. This led them to conduct more than 20 interviews with local residents who had lived through
that history, an experience that further deepened their understanding of
racial injustice. In "A High School Class on Race and Racism," Lawrence
Blum describes how the achievement gap between White students and
students of color can be turned from a dispiriting school problem into a
topic of discussion and analysis in the classroom. What emerges, he argues, can be valuable for students of all races and ethnicities. Racial and
ethnic tensions can also play out through language difference, as Lilia I.
Bartolomé and Pepi Leistyna describe in "Naming and Interrogating Our
English-Only Legacy." In order to understand the racism at the heart of
the English-only movement, they examine the history of European immigrants and, more important, that of indigenous and other "non-White"
linguistic minorities.

Issues of gender and sexuality, no less than of race, ethnicity, and
language, present both challenges and opportunities for teachers—and to
deny the full significance and complexity of gender and sexuality can some-

times impede student development and learning. Kevin K. Kumashiro's essay, "Teaching and Learning Through Desire, Crisis, and Difference: Perverted Reflections on Anti-oppressive Education," opens the section Teaching About Gender and Sexualities. Kumashiro, like many teachers, initially hoped to move his students forward by means of rationality and affirmation, but he soon came to see the ways that uncertainty, even crisis—including the crisis provoked by his coming out as "queer" to his class—can play an essential role in the kind of anti-oppressive education to which he is dedicated. In "Bridging Multicultural Education: Bringing Sexual Orientation into the Children's and Young Adult Literature Classrooms," Patti Capel Swartz argues that lesbian, gay, bisexual, and transgender issues should be included in the curriculum along with those of race, class, and gender; she argues that teachers who remain in the closet may be protecting the very institutions that exclude them, and may also be missing an opportunity to be desperately needed role models for their gay or lesbian students. Swartz offers elementary and middle school teachers an excellent guide to integrating issues of sexuality into their classes. In "Nuns, Midwives, and Witches: Women's Studies in the Elementary Classroom," Sarah Napier shows how feminist college students need not leave their women's studies courses at the door if they enter elementary school teaching. In her classes on the Middle Ages, Napier noticed how talk of kings, castles, and knights excited the boys but left out the girls. In an effort to promote gender equality and to encourage assertive behavior on the part of the girls, Napier introduced nuns, midwives, and witches into the picture.

Our final section, Threats to Public Education: Testing, Tracking, and Privatization, reminds us again of the difficult context within which progressive educators have to work, but it also suggests the possibilities for resistance. In "Leaving Public Education Behind," Stan Karp characterizes the No Child Left Behind Act as an attempt to sell public education to the highest bidder. As NCLB labels schools as failures on the basis of unrealistic standardized tests, demoralizes teachers now pressured to teach to the test, and accelerates teacher turnover, conservative forces hope to justify transferring educational funds into the hands of education management companies and voucher schools, and allow public education simply to sink. In a more positive key, "'I Plan to Be Somebody': The Absence of Tracking Is a Deeply Radical Idea," by Nancy Barnes, describes a college's collaborative project with a Manhattan public high school in which every student, not just a select few, came to campus to take classes. Barnes explains how empowering this practice of nontracking was for students and how instructive for teachers. Far less hopeful, though, is "After Katrina: Tales from a Chartered School Classroom," in which Nicole Polier shows us educational opportunism at its worst. With the New Orleans school system already under pressure, the catastrophe of Hurricane Katrina provided the excuse to back away further from support for public education. Only a handful of schools were reopened, and those as charter schools; students were forced to compete for classrooms and teachers for jobs.

The Epilogue of *Controversies in the Classroom*, however, reminds us of the power we do have as teachers. In "Paulo Freire: On Hope," Kathleen Weiler points out that, as teachers and citizens, we can all too easily lose hope, and our feelings of despair can get passed on to our students as cynicism. She reminds us of the 1960s, when Freire's work helped American teachers to expand and enrich their sense of the possibilities of progressive education, and she calls on him again at a time when perhaps hope is needed even more. Freire, Weiler writes, "never loses sight of this central claim: that the world we live in is the result of human action, that the future will be made by human beings, that history is not static and unchanging, that the oppressive reality we see around us can be transformed." This transformation is our duty as radical teachers, and we believe that this collection can inform, inspire, and give hope to the growing number of teachers invested in the transformative power of education.

Teaching About War

CHAPTER 1

Whose Terrorism?

Bill Bigelow

SHORTLY AFTER the September 11 attacks on the World Trade Center and the Pentagon, President Bush announced these as acts of war and proclaimed a "war on terrorism." But what exactly was to be the target of this war? What precisely did the president mean by terrorism? Despite uttering the words *terror, terrorist,* or *terrorism* 32 times in his September 20 speech to the nation, he never once defined terrorism.

Teachers need to engage our students in a deep critical reading of terms—such as *terrorism, freedom, patriotism,* and *our way of life*—that evoke vivid images but can be used for ambiguous ends.

LESSON ON TERRORISM

I wanted to design a lesson that would get students to surface the definitions of terrorism that they carry around—albeit most likely unconsciously. And I wanted them to apply their definitions to a number of episodes, historical and contemporary, that involved some kind of violence or destruction. I didn't know for certain, but my hunch was that as students applied definitions consistently, they might be able to call into question the "We're Good/They're Bad" dichotomies that have become even more pronounced on the political landscape.

I wrote up several "What Is Terrorism?" scenarios, but instead of using the actual names of countries involved, I substituted fictional names. Given the widespread conflation of patriotism with support for U.S. government policies, I had no confidence that students would be able to label an action taken by their government as "terrorism" unless I attached a pseudonym to each country.

In the following scenario I used the example of U.S. support for the Nicaraguan Contras in the 1980s. "Tobian" is the United States, "Ambar" is Nicaragua, and the country next door is Honduras:

The government of Tobian is very unhappy with the government of Ambar, whose leaders came to power in a revolution that threw out the former Ambar dictator. Tobian decides to do everything in its power to overthrow the new leaders of Ambar. It begins funding a guerrilla army that attacks Ambar from another country next door. Tobian also builds army bases in the next-door country and allows the guerrilla army to use its bases. Tobian supplies almost all the weapons and supplies of the guerrilla army fighting Ambar. The guerrillas generally try to avoid fighting Ambar's army. Instead, they attack clinics, schools, cooperative farms. Sometimes they mine the roads. Many, many civilians are killed and maimed by the Tobian-supported guerrillas. Consistently, the guerrillas raid Ambar and then retreat into the country next door where Tobian has military bases.

Questions: (1) Which, if any, of these activities should be considered "terrorism" according to your definition? (2) Who are the "terrorists"? (3) What more would you need to know to be more sure of your answer?

I knew that in such compressed scenarios lots of important details would be missing; hence, I included question number three to invite students to consider other details that might influence their decisions.

Other scenarios included Israeli soldiers taunting and shooting children in Palestinian refugee camps, with the assistance of U.S. military aid; Indian farmers burning Monsanto-supplied, genetically modified cotton crops and threatening to destroy Monsanto offices; the 1998 U.S. cruise missile attack on Sudan's main pharmaceutical plant; and sanctions against Iraq that, according to UN reports, killed as many as a half million children. The full list of situations can be found at www.rethinkingschools.org/sept11.

DEFINING TERRORISM

As I was on leave, my colleague Sandra Childs invited me into her Franklin High School classroom to teach this lesson to her 11th-grade global studies students. I began by asking students to write down their own personal definitions of terrorism, and to keep these questions in mind: Does terrorism need to involve the killing of many people or can it affect just one person? Can it involve simply the destruction of property, with no injuries? Can governments commit acts of terrorism, or is the term reserved only for people who operate outside of governments? Must terrorism involve the people of one country attacking citizens of another country? Does motive make a difference? Does terrorism need to be intentional?

Immediately following, I explained to students that, in preparation for an activity, I'd like them to get into small groups and read their individual definitions to one another to see if they could build a consensus definition of terrorism. They could choose an exemplary definition from one member or, if they preferred, cobble one together from their separate definitions.

Some groups quickly agreed upon definitions; others would have spent the entire 83-minute class debating definitions if Sandra and I had let them. In most cases, the definitions were simple, but thoughtful. For example: "Intentional acts that create terror, targeted towards a specific group, or innocent people. Not just directly, but indirectly."

I distributed the "What Is Terrorism?" scenarios to students, reviewed the instructions with them, and emphasized that all the scenarios were real. Their main task was to read each situation and to decide whether any of the actions described met their group's definition of terrorism. I gave them permission to approach the situations in whatever order they liked.

Watching students attempt to apply their definitions of terrorism, I was impressed by their eagerness to be consistent. As Sandra and I wandered from group to group, we heard students arguing over whether there was a distinction between oppression and terrorism. Most groups wanted more information on the motives of various actors. Some insisted that if a country supported terrorist acts in another country, then it too was a terrorist; others held that a supporting country could not be held fully responsible for the actions of the actual perpetrators—but if a country knew about terrorism that was enabled with that country's funds and did nothing to prevent it, then it too could be considered guilty of terrorism.

Although this activity was far too involved to be neatly contained in an 83-minute class, by the end many students came to important insights. One student said, "Ever since they announced that we were going to have a war on terrorism I have wondered who or what a terrorist is. And . . . it's suspicious that they still haven't defined terrorism." I asked students why they thought the U.S. government had failed to offer a clear definition of terrorism. One student said, "If you don't have any boundaries, then anyone can be a terrorist." Another said, "The U.S. government won't define terrorism because they don't want to be able to be considered terrorists."

These comments echoed Eqbal Ahmad's insight (1998) that countries that have no intention of being consistent will resist defining terms. As one student wrote after the activity: "I also realized how many terrorism acts the U.S. has committed. When our government doesn't define terrorism, it makes me think that they just want a free shot to kill anyone they want." Wrote another student: "Bush needs to define terrorism in front of our nation before he does anything else, and then he needs to stick with the definition, not bend it to suit the U.S."

But then there was this student comment: "I, myself, am really tired of hearing about it. If I go to war, so what, I'll fight for my country. What does this have to do with global studies?" And this young man: "I feel if we don't get our revenge against these 'terrorists' it will diminish the trust of our nation towards our government."

These remarks reminded me of being in the classroom during the fall of 1990, after Iraq had invaded Kuwait and the United States was assembling its military attack force. Many students resisted critical analysis, sensing that critique eroded the "patriotic" unity then building in the country—that appending a "not so fast" onto the flag waving interrupted a sense of collective purpose that felt good to many of them. At least that was how I read some students' resistance. During times of war, students may regard even the mildest critical examination of government policy as unpatriotic or even subversive. Nonetheless, I was impressed by how many students in Sandra's classes appeared eager to question their government's framing of key issues.

As we wrapped up in one class, Sandra asked a wonderful question: "What difference do you think it would make if students all over the country were having the discussion that we're having today?"

There were two quick answers before the bell rang: "I'd feel a lot better about the U.S.," and "I think we'd lose a lot of people who'd want to go fight for the country."

My interpretation: The more students understand about the exercise of U.S. power in the world—both military and economic—the less likely they are to want to extend it.

ECONOMIC TERRORISM

After I'd used the "What Is Terrorism?" situations with Sandra's classes, I realized that, with the exception of sanctions, all of them were incidents of direct attacks on civilians or property. Did my examples narrow students' consideration of "terrorism"?

In her article "Solidarity Against All Forms of Terrorism," Indian environmentalist and scholar Vandana Shiva (2001) urges us to embrace a more expansive notion of terrorism. She asks us to consider "economic policies which push people into poverty and starvation as a form of terrorism," such as International Monetary Fund/World Bank–mandated structural adjustment programs that force governments to cut food and medical programs, with the full knowledge of the misery this will engender. Shiva writes:

> [In India,] 50 million tribals who have been flooded out of their homes by dams over the past 4 decades were also victims of terrorism—they have faced the terror of technology and destructive development. The whole world repeatedly watched the destruction of the World Trade Center towers, but the destruction of millions of sacred shrines and homes and farms by forces of injustice, greed, and globalization go unnoticed. (Shiva, 2001)

To help students consider whether some situations could be considered economic terrorism, I've added several new "What Is Terrorism?" scenarios. One deals with deaths from AIDS in southern Africa, where, for instance, international banks have forced the Zambian government to pay annual debt service charges greater than spending on health and education combined and where, according to the United Nations, life expectancy will soon drop to 33 years, a level not seen in the Western world since medieval times. Another new scenario focuses on transnational corporations that knowingly pay wages that are insufficient to sustain life.

TERRORISM'S GHOSTS

The U.S. government is ill placed to lecture the world about terrorism, especially when it has never bothered to define it. Writing in the British daily *The Guardian*, Indian novelist Arundhati Roy offered the perspective of an individual who is on the receiving end of U.S. global power:

> The Sept. 11 attacks were a monstrous calling card from a world gone horribly wrong. The message may have been written by bin Laden (who knows?) and delivered by his couriers, but it could well have been signed by the ghosts of the victims of America's old wars. The millions killed in Korea, Vietnam and Cambodia, the 17,500 killed when Israel—backed by the U.S.—invaded Lebanon in 1982, the 200,000 Iraqis killed in Operation Desert Storm, the thousands of Palestinians who have died fighting Israel's occupation of the West Bank. And the millions who died, in Yugoslavia, Somalia, Haiti, Chile, Nicaragua, El Salvador, the Dominican Republic, Panama, at the hands of all the terrorists, dictators and genocidists whom the American government supported, trained, bankrolled and supplied with arms. And this is far from being a comprehensive list. (Roy, 2001)

It's not our role as teachers to climb on our soapbox to rail about U.S. foreign policy. And yet without an honest examination of events like those listed by Roy, how can we expect students to maintain any critical perspective on the U.S. "war against terrorism"? Let's clarify with students what precisely we mean by terrorism. And then let's encourage students to apply this definition to U.S. conduct in the world.

Underlying this curricular demand for consistency is the basic democratic, indeed human, premise that the lives of people from one nation are not worth more than the lives of people from another. A Pakistani university student, Nabil Ahmed, expressed this sentiment to the *Christian Science Monitor*: "There is only one way for America to be a friend of Islam. And that is if they consider our lives to be as precious as their own" (Ford, 2001).

APPENDIX: HANDOUT FOR STUDENT DISCUSSIONS

Instructions: Based on the definitions of terrorism that your group came up with, decide (1) which of the situations below are "terrorism," (2) who the "terrorists" are in the situation, and (3) what additional information you would need to know to be more sure of your answers. All the situations below are true, but the names of countries and peoples have been changed. It may help your group to make a diagram of some of the situations.

Situations

1. Soldiers from the country of Marak surround a refugee camp made up of people from the country of Bragan. The refugee camp is crowded and the people there are extremely poor. Most of the Bragan people in the refugee camp hate the army of Marak, believing that Marak has invaded Bragan, has taken all the best land and resources for themselves, and treats people from Bragan very poorly. Young men in the refugee camp sometimes fire guns at the soldiers.

   According to an eyewitness, a reporter from the *New York Times*, Marak soldiers use loudspeakers to call insults into the refugee camp—in the Bragan language. Over the loudspeakers, soldiers shout obscenities and things like "Son of a whore!" They dare young Bragan boys—sometimes as young as 10 or 11—to come out near the electric fence that separates the refugee camp from a wealthy settlement of Marak citizens. When the boys and young men go near the fence to throw stones or yell at the Marak soldiers, the soldiers use silencers and fire on the boys with live ammunition, often killing or maiming them. In an article, the *New York Times* reporter expressed horror at what he witnessed. He wrote: "Children have been shot in other conflicts I have covered—death squads gunned them down in El Salvador and Guatemala, mothers with infants were lined up and massacred in Algeria, and Serb snipers put children in their sights and watched them crumple onto the pavement in Sarajevo—but I have never before watched soldiers entice children like mice into a trap and murder them for sport." The government of Marak clearly knows about the behavior of their soldiers and does nothing to stop them. Indeed, Marak soldiers so regularly taunt citizens of Bragan that this behavior appears to be the policy of the Marak government. One additional fact: Every year, Marak is given enormous amounts of money and military equipment by the country of Bolaire, which is aware of how these are used by Marak.

2. Farmers from the country of Belveron are angry at their own government and at a corporation from the country of Paradar. The Belveron government has allowed the Paradar corporation to plant "test" crops of genetically engineered cotton. The genetically engineered crops produce their own pesticide. Many Belveron farmers worry that the genetically engineered crops will pollute their crops—as has happened many times in other countries—and will lead to a breed of superpests that will be immune to chemical pesticides and also to the organic pest control methods many poor farmers use. Without growing and selling cotton, the farmers have no way to feed their families. Belveron farmers also believe that the Paradar corporation does not really care about them, but instead cares only for its own profit. They believe that the corporation wants to get Belveron farmers "addicted" to genetically engineered cotton seeds—which the corporation has patented—so that the corporation will have a monopoly. Belveron farmers further point out that the corporation has not told farmers that the "tests" on their land may be risky and could pollute their non–genetically engineered cotton crops.

   Belveron farmers have announced that they will burn to the ground all the genetically engineered cotton crops. They hope to drive the Paradar corporation out of Belveron. Belveron farmers have also threatened that they may destroy the offices of the Paradar corporation.

3. The army of Kalimo has invaded the country of Iona, next door. There are a number of refugee camps in Iona with thousands of people living in them. The refugees themselves lost their homes many years before. Some lost them in wars with Kalimo; others were forced out of their homes by Kalimo. The area around the refugee camps is controlled by the Kalimo army. The commander of the Kalimo army sealed off the

refugee camps and allowed militias from Iona, who are hostile to the refugees, to enter two refugee camps and slaughter hundreds of people. The killing went on for 40 hours. At least 1,800 people were murdered, perhaps more. One additional fact: The army of Kalimo receives a great deal of military aid from the country of Terramar. Terramar learned of the massacre of the refugees in Iona, but did not halt military aid to Kalimo.

4. A corporation based in the country of Menin has a chemical factory located in the much poorer country of Pungor. One night, huge amounts of poisonous gases from the factory begin spewing out into the area around the factory. Nobody outside the factory was warned because someone in the company had turned off the safety siren. Not until the gas was upon residents in their beds, searing their eyes, filling their mouths and lungs, did the communities surrounding the factory know of their danger. According to one report: "Gasping for breath and near blind, people stampeded into narrow alleys. In the mayhem children were torn from the hands of their mothers, never to see them again. Those who still could were screaming. Some were wracked with seizures and fell under trampling feet. Some, stumbling in a sea of gas, their lungs on fire, were drowned in their own bodily fluids." No one knows how many people died, but perhaps as many as 6,000 that night and in the years after, more than 10,000.

   The corporation had begun a cost-cutting drive prior to the disaster: lowering training periods for operatives, using low-cost materials, adopting hazardous operating procedures, cutting the number of operatives in half. A confidential company audit prior to the accident had identified 61 hazards. Nothing was done.

   After the tragedy, the corporation concentrated on avoiding liability, sending in its legal team days before a medical team. Company officials lied about the poisonous nature of the chemicals at the plant. To this day the corporation refuses to disclose medical information on the leaked gases, maintaining it to be a "trade secret." The company did pay some of the victims' families. On average, victims received less than $350 from the company—a total loss of 48 cents per share of company stock.

   Conditions in this Pungor community are still hazardous: soil and water are still heavily contaminated. Mercury has been found at between 20,000 and 6 million times the expected levels. In this community, the rate of stillborn infants is three times the national average of Pungor; infant mortality is twice as high as the national average.

5. The government of Tobian is very unhappy with the government of Ambar, whose leaders came to power in a revolution that threw out

the former Ambar dictator. Tobian decides to overthrow the new leaders of Ambar. They begin funding a guerrilla army that will attack Ambar from another country next door. So Tobian builds army bases in the next-door country and allows the guerrilla army to use its bases. Almost all the weapons and supplies of the guerrilla army are supplied by Tobian. The guerrillas generally try to avoid fighting the army of Ambar. Instead they attack clinics, schools, cooperative farms. Sometimes they mine the roads. Many, many civilians are killed and maimed by the Tobian-supported guerrillas. The guerrillas raid into Ambar and then retreat into the country next door where Tobian has military bases.

6. Simultaneously, the embassies of the country of Anza in two other countries were bombed. In one country, 213 people were killed and more than 1,000 injured; in the other, 11 people were killed and at least 70 injured. In retaliation, about 3 weeks later, Anza launched missiles at the capital city of Baltus, destroying a pharmaceutical factory and injuring at least 10 people, and killing one. Anza claimed that this factory was manufacturing chemicals that could be used to make VX nerve gas—although Anza offered no substantial proof of this claim. Anza also claimed that a prominent individual whom they link to the embassy bombings was connected to the pharmaceutical factory, although they provided no evidence of this claim, either—and a great deal of evidence exists to prove that there is no link. Baltus pointed out that 2 years earlier they expelled the prominent individual, and vigorously denied that the pharmaceutical plant was producing nerve gas agents. They said that this was an important factory, producing 70% of the needed medicines for the people of Baltus—including vital medicines to treat malaria and tuberculosis. They allowed journalists and other diplomats to visit the factory to verify that no chemical weapons were being produced there. Journalists and others who visited the factory agreed that the destroyed factory appeared to be producing only medicines. It is not known how many people may have died in Baltus for lack of the medicines that were being produced in that factory. Anza blocked the United Nations from launching the investigation demanded by Baltus.

7. At least 1 million people in the country of Lukin are infected with HIV/AIDS. Between 1991 and 2001, 700,000 people died of AIDS in Lukin. Currently, about 300 people die each day of AIDS-related causes. Largely because of the HIV/AIDS crisis, life expectancy in Lukin is expected to drop from 43 to 33 years, a level last experienced in Europe in medieval times. AIDS could be controlled with a combination of drugs, frequently called a drug "cocktail," including AZT. However, given current drug prices, this could cost as much as $18,000 a year per patient.

This year, Lukin will pay $174 million in interest payments on its debt—most of which will go to two large international banks. This debt was incurred many years ago, by a different government from the current one. The loans were pushed by banks, which had huge amounts of money to lend because oil-producing countries had deposited so much of their revenue into these banks. As one observer put it, "The banks were hot to get in. All the banks . . . stepped forward. They showed no foresight. They didn't do any credit analysis. It was wild."

Loans benefited mostly bankers and the rich of Lukin. However, most people in Lukin are poor—the gross national product (GNP) per capita is $350. The $174 million in interest payments is more than the money Lukin will spend on health care and education combined. Money that could go to pay for AIDS prevention and therapies for people with AIDS instead is being sent to banks in so-called developed countries.

The international banks know about the dire health situation in Lukin. They have allowed Lukin to postpone some debts—but only after Lukin agreed to certain conditions set by the banks that gave the banks greater control over Lukin's economy, for example, requiring Lukin to sell its national bank to private investors. Still, so long as the banks force Lukin to pay interest on its debts, there is no way Lukin can deal effectively with the AIDS crisis. Three hunderd people a day continue to die.

8. Led by the country of Lomandia, the United Nations waged a war against the country of Moretta, saying that Moretta illegally invaded another nearby country. After Moretta's army was defeated and removed from the country it had invaded, Lomandia pushed for "sanctions" against Moretta, until Moretta could prove that it was not engaged in a program to produce "weapons of mass destruction," such as nuclear bombs or poison gas. The sanctions meant that Moretta was not allowed to buy or sell almost anything from other countries in the world. Moretta could not get spare parts to repair water purification plants damaged by bombing during the war. It could not get medicines and spare parts for medical equipment. Moretta claimed that it allowed inspections from the United Nations, but Lomandia says that it did not. According to the United Nations perhaps a half million children died as a result of the sanctions. Documents from Lomandia show that it knew that Moretta civilians were dying as a result of waterborne diseases. When asked in a television interview about the reports of massive numbers of civilian deaths—perhaps as many as a half million children over several years—a high government official from Lomandia

said: "I think that is a very hard choice, but the price, we think, the price is worth it."

9. Bartavia is considered by many to be one of the most repressive countries in the world, especially if you are not White. Only Whites can vote; only Whites can travel freely; only Whites can live where they like. Most Whites live comfortably, even luxuriously. Conditions for people who are not White are some of the worst in the world. Bartavia imprisons people who organize for change. Torture is widespread. Over the years, there have been numerous massacres of non-White Bartavia civilians—sometimes of young children. The main organizations working for change in Bartavia have asked the world not to invest money in Bartavia and not to have economic or cultural relations with the country until it commits itself to change. Nonetheless, many countries continue to do business with Bartavia. One in particular, Sarino, has allowed its corporations to increase their investments in Bartavia from $150 million to $2.5 billion—all this during a period of tremendous violence and discrimination. Who knows how many thousands of people have been killed—through guns or poverty—as a result of Sarino's actions.

10. The Sport-King Corporation produces athletic equipment sold all over the world. Although the headquarters of Sport-King is in the country of Morcosas, all its products are manufactured in other countries. Sport-King contracts with subcontractors to make its products. More than 500,000 people, mostly women, work for these subcontractors in poor countries.

     Sport-King has a "code of conduct," which is supposed to ensure that workers are not mistreated by Sport-King's subcontractors. For example, no child laborers are supposed to be hired, no prisoners may be used as workers, workers may not be forced to work more than 60 hours a week, and so on. Sport-King's "code of conduct" specifies that workers must be paid a country's "minimum wage." However, it does not say that this minimum wage needs to be a living wage. Even poor-country governments admit that the minimum wage is not enough for people to live on. Sport-King says that it pays the legal wage, but it knows that not all its workers can survive on this wage.

     Companies like Sport-King locate their factories in countries that don't allow unions, that outlaw strikes, and that jail workers who demand higher pay and better conditions. In fact, Sport-King chooses to locate its factories in some of the most repressive countries in the world. Human rights groups argue that companies like Sport-King knowingly locate their factories in very repressive places so that workers can more easily be controlled and exploited. These human rights groups argue that companies like Sport-King could easily afford to pay their workers living wages, but because this would come out of their enormous profits they choose not to.

What Is Terrorism? Who Are the Terrorists?

Who's who:

Situation 1. The country of Marak is Israel. Bragan is Palestine. Bolaire is the United States. This particular example is taken from "A Gaza Diary," by Chris Hedges in the October 2001 *Harpers.*

Situation 2. The country of Belveron is India. Paradar is the United States. The corporation is Monsanto.

Situation 3. Kalimo is Israel. Iona is Lebanon. Terramar is the United States. The refugees are Palestinian. The camps were Sabra and Shatila in 1982. The militia was Christian Phalangist.

Situation 4. The country of Menin is the United States. Pungor is India. The corporation was Union Carbide, in Bhopal, India. The year was 1985.

Situation 5. The country of Tobian is the United States. Ambar is Nicaragua. The country next door is Honduras. The time is the 1980s during the U.S.-sponsored Contra war.

Situation 6. The country of Anza is the United States. Baltus is Sudan. The countries where the U.S. embassies were bombed are Kenya and Tanzania. The prominent individual mentioned is Osama bin Laden.

Situation 7. The country of Lukin is Zambia. The banks are the International Monetary Fund and the World Bank.

Situation 8. The country of Lomandia is the United States. Moretta is Iraq. The U.S. official quoted was Madeleine Albright, then U.S. ambassador to the United Nations, later secretary of state. She was interviewed on *60 Minutes* by Leslie Stahl in 1996.

Situation 9. The country of Bartavia is South Africa during apartheid. Sarino is the United States.

Situation 10. Sport-King is Nike, although it could be many transnational corporations. And the country of Morcosas is the United States.

NOTE

This essay first appeared in "War, Terrorism, and Our Classrooms, "a special issue of *Rethinking Schools* magazine, Winter 2001–2. We are grateful to *Rethinking Schools* for permission to reprint this article. To subscribe to *Rethinking Schools*, go to www.rethinkingschools.org. To access the full special issue, "War, Terrorism, and

Our Classrooms," visit Rethinking Schools online at: http://www.rethinkingschools
.org/special_reports/sept11/index.shtml

REFERENCES

Ahmad, E. (1998, October 12). *Terrorism: Theirs and ours.* Speech at the University of Colorado, Boulder.

Ford, P. (2001, September 27). Why do they hate us? *Christian Science Monitor.* Retrieved March 8, 2008, from http://www.csmonitor.com/2001/0927/p1s1-wogi.html

Roy, A. (2001, September 29). The algebra of infinite justice. *Guardian.* Retrieved March 8, 2008, from www.guardian.co.uk/Archive/Article0,4273,4266289,00.html

Shiva, V. (2001, September 18). Solidarity against all forms of terrorism. Retrieved March 8, 2008, from http://www.zmag.org/shivacalam2.htm

CHAPTER 2

Can Vietnam Awaken Us Again?
Teaching the Literature of the Vietnam War

H. Bruce Franklin

WE MUST NEVER forget that the Vietnam War created the most powerful antiwar movement in history. Even the Modern Language Association was shaken to its roots, making it sprout such forbidden fruit as the Radical Caucus.[1] The war and the movement against it transformed American culture and consciousness so deeply that our rulers have been forced to spend decades erasing memory and refilling it with fantasies, myths, illusions, and lies. These falsifications are necessary for the sweeping militarization of American culture, essential to our current epoch of endless imperial warfare.

President George Bush the First was remarkably frank about the need to brainwash us. As he explained in his 1989 inaugural address, the problem is that we still retain our memory: "The final lesson of Vietnam is that no great nation can long afford to be sundered by a memory." What Bush meant by "Vietnam" by then was already no longer a country or even a war. Vietnam was something that had happened to us, an event that had divided, wounded, and victimized America. As the grotesque title of one widely adopted history textbook puts it: *Vietnam: An American Ordeal*.[2]

In that 1989 inaugural speech, Bush explicitly blamed "Vietnam" for all the "divisiveness" in America and the lack of trust in our government. Just 2 years later, gloating over what seemed America's glorious defeat of Iraq, he jubilantly boasted to a nation festooned in jingoist yellow ribbons, "By God, we've kicked the Vietnam syndrome once and for all!" ("Kicking," 1991, p. A-1).

The "Vietnam syndrome" had entered America's cultural vocabulary in a 1980 campaign speech by Ronald Reagan, the same speech in which he redefined the Vietnam War as "a noble cause" (Isaacs, 1997, p. 49:

Turner, 1996, p. 63). By the late 1970s, the Vietnamese were already being transformed into fiendish torturers of heroic American POWs. By the mid-1990s, they were becoming erased from the picture altogether. Want a snapshot of the cultural progression from the late 1970s to the mid-1990s? The Academy Award for Best Picture of 1978 went to *The Deer Hunter*, which systematically replaced crucial images from the Vietnam War with their precise opposites, meticulously reversing the roles of victims and victimizers. The Academy Award for Best Picture of 1994 went to *Forrest Gump*, which projects Vietnam as merely an uninhabited jungle that for inscrutable reasons shoots at nice American boys who happen to be passing through. And from then on, one loveable American icon would be Gump, someone incapable of knowing or understanding history.

With the erasure of history came the reign of fantasy: a war fought with one hand behind our back; an invasion of the democratic nation of "South Vietnam" by the communists of "North Vietnam"; betrayal by the liberal media, pinko professors, and Jane Fonda; returning veterans spat upon by hippies; hundreds of POWs forsaken after the war to be tortured for decades; and so on.

Emerging from the quarter century of post–Vietnam War American fantasy are the students sitting in our college classrooms today. That fantasy lives inside their minds, its myths and phony images filtering and obscuring their vision of history, of America's actions in today's world, and even of themselves. This should not be looked upon as merely an impediment to education, or worse still, some infection to be cured with a dose of counterbrainwashing brainwashing.

Why? Because these students are in some senses the world's greatest experts on late 20th-century and early 21st-century American culture. They bring into the classroom invaluable experience and potential expertise on the current cultural role of "Vietnam." For them, the words *Vietnam* and *the sixties* are powerful, complex, and disquieting signifiers. Precisely because those signifiers have become so falsified, today's students are potentially capable of experiencing something close to what millions of us experienced during the war: a direct confrontation with one's own false consciousness. For many of us, this was the most literally radicalizing experience, because it made us understand the very roots of our own perception of historical and cultural reality. We realized that we had indeed been brainwashed, and we learned who did it and why. We comprehended how 1950s American culture had made the Vietnam War possible. For many of us involved in the genesis of the Modern Language Association's Radical Caucus, we even began to see how this culture had determined how we had been reading and teaching literature, and even which literature we had been choosing to read and teach, and so we began to change our ways.

Well, we cannot very well load our students into a time machine so they can relive our Vietnam-era experience. However, that experience still lives on in forms that dynamically interact with American culture today. In response to the Vietnam War, America produced and continues to produce two great and wonderful achievements. The first is the antiwar movement itself, which is renewing its powers at this very historical moment. The second is a tremendous body of literature flowing out of the war and the consciousness it transformed. That literature—including fiction, poetry, memoir, songs, and film—exists today, continues to develop, and can act as an astonishingly effective agent of transformation. Maybe it's the closest thing we have to a time machine that can carry knowledge backward and forward from the Vietnam War to today's forever war.

Based on my own experience teaching a course on the Vietnam War and American culture for more than 20 years, I am convinced that no other literature has anything approaching this transformative force.[3] A revealing—and encouraging—sign of our times is the fact that this course, like similar courses around the country, is always overenrolled. But teachers do not need an entire course to share the impact of this literature with students. Introduced into any course exploring contemporary literature, it contextualizes almost all the other works created from the mid-1960s to the present—because the Vietnam War forms such a crucial part of the matrix of all contemporary literature.

Vietnam War literature profoundly affects today's students because of its confrontation with their own false consciousness, because it casts such glaring light on our current crisis, and because "Vietnam" has such lingering and puzzling meaning for them. Anyone growing up in America in the past couple of decades probably has sensed the emotional temperature rising whenever the term *Vietnam* has been used in any group of adult Americans. Many of my students have fathers, uncles, or other relatives who fought in the war. Often this makes the subject taboo in their homes, thus arousing the usual human curiosity about forbidden zones. Many students are also drawn to what is known as "the sixties," which for some evokes a strange nostalgia. As one young woman put it, "I wish that I were the same age I am now in the sixties."

Some are deeply involved in the music of the period, which includes some important antiwar literature. For example, one student, a Creedence Clearwater Revival (CCR) fanatic, had a collection that included all their concerts and releases in every form—from 45s to CDs. He adamantly refused to believe that "Fortunate Son" was an antiwar song, until he saw it confirmed directly on John Fogarty's Web site. Then the student wrote a wonderful essay describing how this forced him to rethink his understanding of CCR and thus his own acculturation.

Vietnam veterans have an exalted place in today's pantheon of American heroes, sanctified by that myth of the spat-upon veteran. The literature by Vietnam veterans, unprecedented in scale and depth of insight, has amazing effects on students.

One text by a Vietnam veteran affects students more profoundly than any work of any kind I have taught in more than 4 decades in university classrooms. That is *Passing Time*, a memoir by W. D. Ehrhart (1995), which makes readers participate in his own transformation from a gung-ho anti-Communist who enlisted in the Marines at the age of 17 and served two tours in Vietnam into a radical visionary artist. Once, when I walked into class the day the book was due, there was an odd hubbub. One conservative young man, who had attended military school and was planning to be a career military officer—and who had been arguing vociferously with me all semester—seemed especially upset. Suddenly he blurted out: "I've never read a book like this. It's changing my whole life." The next thing I knew, he was up in front of the class saying, "We've got to have this guy come talk with us. Why don't we kick in to get whatever it takes to bring him." There was a chorus of assent. Someone called out from the back, "Let's each put in $5." Someone else yelled, "Five dollars? It costs $7.50 just to see a movie." (This was in 1993.) "OK," said a new voice, "let's make it $10." And so these students, almost all of whom work to be able to afford college, contributed ten dollars apiece to get a visit from W. D. Ehrhart.

When I assigned *Passing Time* in a graduate seminar, five graduate students independently decided to assign the book in their freshman composition sections. All reported that it was by far the most effective and best-liked text in their course.

Ehrhart's deep probing of his own consciousness and of American history helps prepare for that great text about memory and denial, Tim O'Brien's (1994) *In the Lake of the Woods*. This is such a demanding book that I was quite hesitant about assigning it to my students, who have not been well prepared for sophisticated reading. But again and again, I see it work as a breakthrough text, as students become absorbed in its psychological, historical, and philosophical challenges. For many, the novel makes the My Lai massacre a crucial nexus between what O'Brien calls "story truth" and "happening truth," and a devastating revelation of the horrors America is inflicting on the world and itself. Introduced as the sole Vietnam War text into my course "Crime and Punishment in American Literature," *In the Lake of the Woods* brings home with full force the devastating and timely issue of crimes committed by a nation, particularly our own nation.

This year offers a special opportunity for teaching Vietnam War literature as an awakening. Almost a half century ago, Graham Greene's *The Quiet
American* foresaw how America, convinced of its own righteousness, preach-
ing democracy and spewing bombs, might bathe the world in blood for
decades to come. Greene saw the quiet American, affable and amiable, ar-
mored with innocence and the best intentions, as the archetypal terrorist of
our epoch. When the novel appeared in 1955, it was savaged by the critical
establishment. In 1958 the novel was made into a movie that turned Greene's
message into its exact opposite: exalting anticommunism and American
political missionary zeal, the movie was dedicated explicitly to the puppet
America had installed to rule Vietnam. But in 2002, *The Quiet American* was
made into another film, one faithful to Greene's vision. After September 11,
Miramax Films tried to deep-six the movie, but it has risen like the phoe-
nix, opening widely in early 2003. The film makes a perfect bridge back to
the novel, allowing its message to travel forward a half century into our own
era, with its terrifying enactment of Greene's prophetic vision.

Poetry by Vietnam veterans not only explodes the phony history of
the war but also demystifies poetry itself. Marilyn McMahon's (1988/1996)
devastating poem "Knowing" obliquely illuminates Washington's professed
outrage about Iraq's chemical weapons by reminding us of the most in-
tensive chemical warfare in human history, that used by the United States
in Vietnam. As a combat nurse, she knew that the stated purpose of "de-
foliation" was destroying "the hiding places of snipers / and ambushing
guerrillas," but she did not know "the price" until all the nurses with whom
she served had either multiple miscarriages or children with deformities
or cancer. The poem concludes:

> I knew what I would never know,
> What the poisons and my fears
> have removed forever from my knowing,
> The conceiving, the carrying of a child,
> the stretching of my womb, my breasts.
> The pain of labor.
> The bringing forth from my body a new life.
>
> I choose not to know
> if my eggs are
> misshapen and withered
> as the trees along the river.
> If snipers are hidden
> in the coils of my DNA.

Let me conclude with a 14-line poem by Steve Hassett (1976/1996),
who served as a paratrooper in the First Air Cavalry:

AND WHAT WOULD YOU DO, MA?

And what would you do, ma,
if eight of your sons step
out of the TV and begin
killing chickens and burning
hooches in the living room,
stepping on booby traps
and dying in the kitchen,
beating your husband and
taking him and shooting
skag and forgetting in
the bathroom?
would you lock up your daughter?
would you stash the apple pie?
would you change channels?

NOTES

Originally presented on December 28, 2002, to the Radical Caucus at the Modern Language Association Convention, this chapter will (alas) probably be relevant for quite a while to come.

1. For an instructive history, see the introduction to Kampf & Lauter, 1972.

2. This 1990 text written by George Donelson Moss and published by Prentice-Hall, a subsidiary of Viacom, had gone through three editions by 1998. Among the important studies that have explored how the war has been transformed into a trauma inflicted not by America on Vietnam but by Vietnam on America, see Beattie, 1998; Jeffords, 1989; and Turner, 1996.

3. My "Vietnam and America" course began in 1980, just as the war was being redefined as a "noble cause." The course is described in Franklin, 1981, an article that instantly generated a firestorm of criticism but also helped initiate courses at other institutions. To provide a historical text for the courses burgeoning in the mid-1980s, Marvin Gettleman, Jane Franklin, Marilyn Young, and I edited *Vietnam and America* (Franklin, Franklin, Gettleman, & Young, 1984; rev. ed., 1995). In 1996, I edited *The Vietnam War in American Stories, Songs, and Poems* (Franklin, 1996), which brings together a wide range of stories and poems, many by veterans, as well as some of the most popular and influential songs about the war, from Country Joe to Bruce Springsteen.

REFERENCES

Beattie, K. (1998). *The scar that binds: American culture and the Vietnam War*. New York: New York University Press.

Ehrhart, W. D. (1995). *Passing time: Memoir of a Vietnam veteran against the war* (2nd ed.). Amherst: University of Massachusetts Press.

Franklin, B. (1981, November 4). Teaching Vietnam today: Who won, and why? *Chronicle of Higher Education, 23*(10), 64.

Franklin, B. (Ed.). (1996). *The Vietnam War in American stories, songs, and poems.* Boston: Bedford Books/St. Martin's.

Franklin, B., Franklin, J., Gettleman, M., & Young, M. (Eds.). (1984). *Vietnam and America: A documented history.* New York: Grove/Atlantic.

Hassett, S. (1996). And what would you do, ma. In B. Franklin (Ed.), *The Vietnam War in American stories, songs, and poems* (p. 2). Boston: Bedford/St. Martins. (Original work published 1976)

Isaacs, A. R. (1997). *Vietnam shadows: The war, its ghost, and its legacy.* Baltimore: Johns Hopkins University Press.

Jeffords, S. (1989). *The remasculinization of America: Gender and the Vietnam War.* Bloomington: Indiana University Press.

Kampf, L., & Lauter, P. (Eds.). (1972). *The politics of literature: Dissenting essays in the teaching of English.* New York: Random House.

Kicking the "Vietnam syndrome." (1991, March 4). *Washington Post,* p. A-1.

McMahon, M. (1996). Knowing. In B. Franklin (Ed.), *The Vietnam War in American stories, songs, and poems* (pp. 277–279). Boston: Bedford/St. Martins. (Original work published 1988)

Moss, G. D. (1998). *Vietnam: An American ordeal* (3rd ed.). Upper Saddle River, NJ: Prentice Hall.

O'Brien, T. (1994). *In the Lake of the Woods.* Boston: Houghton Mifflin.

Turner, F. (1996). *Echoes of combat: The Vietnam War in American memory.* New York: Doubleday.

CHAPTER 3

Dialogues About 9/11, the Media, and Race: Lessons from a Secondary Classroom

Rita Verma

TEACHING DURING a time of war and after 9/11 requires new ways of integrating themes of social justice, peace education, and reflective thinking into our pedagogy. How have middle school and high school students in particular responded to 9/11 and the war on terrorism? Teachers play an important role in stimulating constructive dialogue with students on these topics, but the curriculum that is generally available to K–12 educators on 9/11 is limited and may conspicuously leave out dialogue on anti-immigrant racism. As a teacher of South Asian origin, I have experienced racism since 9/11 firsthand, and I have observed trends in television, radio, and print media that saturate popular culture with images of terror and war and encourage racial stereotyping. These experiences prompted me to spend some time in my own middle school classroom trying to break the silence and foster critical discussion on the topic of racial stereotyping and social justice in a time of war. In this chapter I will reflect upon my experiences teaching the unit and its impact on school culture.

9/11 MEDIA IMAGES AND POPULAR CULTURE

Since 9/11, media images have established the suspect and dangerous "Other" as a brown-skinned, bearded, turbaned male terrorist. This image of terror has most obviously been associated with Osama bin Laden, but it also reflects a broader anti-immigrant ethos wrapped around cultural and religious symbols that have nothing to do with terrorism. In the case of images of the East, the Third World, or specifically Arab nations, media culture has been engaging in a dramatic spectacle and a disinformation campaign that dehumanizes and victimizes Arabs and portrays stereotypical images of the "civilized West" and "barbaric Arabs" that further become part of an oppressive hegemonic discourse. Rallying and mobilizing fear of this fabricated vision of evil, these representations contribute to a discourse of violence against Arabs and others who resemble them.

The Sikh community, in particular, has been victimized by hate crimes after 9/11. The case of Balvinder Singh Sodhi is a prominent example. In the aftermath of 9/11, Sodhi, a gas station owner in Mesa, Arizona, was killed by three men who pulled up in pickup trucks and shot him three times. The murder was later determined to be a hate crime. There are thousands of examples of harassment, assault, garbage throwing, pushing, and shoving documented by Sikh watch groups. In schools across the country, students have reported incidents of harassment, violence, and name-calling. Other South Asian communities have reported incidents of harassment as well. Horrific media images that spur fear and hate are amplified by politicians and authority figures, whose commentaries encourage and validate violence and hostile attitudes toward targeted communities. Senator James Cooksey, for example, has called Sikhs, who wear turbans, "towelheads" and "diaperheads." Popular talk show hosts such as David Letterman make bad jokes about Sikh cab drivers as well. Such comments only accentuate difficulties in making America "home" for certain immigrant communities. They shape the images that Americans hold about Arabs, Arab Americans, and other religious, ethnic, and immigrant groups. The fact that there was a sharp rise in hate crimes against Arabs, Sikhs, and South Asians after 9/11 is a measure of what the public learned to view as a threat. The victims of hate crimes have ranged from youngsters in school to elders in the communities. These complex social processes have become sites of struggle in schools as well, where new incidents of harassment and violence are cause for concern.

What is taught in the classroom can have a positive effect in interrupting stereotypes and assumptions about ethnic groups. Painting a more accurate picture of what is happening in the world and understanding the complexity of issues such as terrorism, immigration, and cultural difference are integral to achieving this goal. Yet the limited resources and prescriptive curriculum of most schools require educators to be creative in engaging students in such discussions. Values, cultural forms, and traditional knowledge that originate from a Eurocentric perspective form "core knowledge" and create limitations in curriculum. The celebration of core knowledge also excludes the voices and experiences of the immigrant communities of South Asia and the Middle East. For example, Cameron McCarthy, in *The Uses of Culture: Education and the Limits of Ethnic Affiliation* (1998), states that the production and negative depictions of the Third

World in textbooks draw on media language that is powerful and saturates popular culture both in and outside of school. Readings and lessons on the Middle East and South Asia are often excluded or form a minimal part of the curriculum. Moreover, there is a significant failure to disrupt emerging stereotypes. With the absence of an informative curriculum about the factual histories of peoples of the Middle East and South Asia, Sikh and South Asian students (especially those who wear turbans), as well as Arab Americans, in many ways become forced to "teach" fellow students about their ethnic backgrounds.

DISCUSSIONS IN THE CLASSROOM

My experience in a suburban school in eastern New York demonstrates the manner in which anti-immigrant media language pervades popular culture in this particular school. In this middle school, the student population is diverse in terms of ethnicity and socioeconomic status, which led me to hope that diverse perspectives would liven up discussions on race and social justice, especially in the aftermath of 9/11. The ethnic breakdown of the school is 60% Caucasian, 16% African American, 19% Latino, 3% Asian American, and 2% Other. Students come from different socioeconomic backgrounds, from affluent middle class to lower middle class. Parental occupations range from business owners, attorneys, and doctors to store clerks, domestic help, and unemployed. However, I soon came to realize that the majority of the students, despite this economic and cultural diversity, expressed discomfort in regard to immigrants of Arab and South Asian backgrounds. This discomfort was expressed equally by White, Latino, and African American students.

In the short aftermath of 9/11 there was a brief moment in our school when teachers and students came together and created a memorial in the form of a bulletin board to commemorate and promise never to forget the tragedy and its victims. The bulletin board included newspaper clippings of the twin towers, pictures of Osama bin Laden, images of men in turbans, and words such as "terror," "fear," and "war." This bulletin board was regarded as a "great work" and a wonderful way to remember by school staff. Students passed by this visual display day in and day out and its images served to "teach" about that tragic day. "Unspoken" tragedies excluded from this memorial included the intensifying of stereotyping and fear of, and antagonism toward, groups of people who seemed somehow associated with the images of terror. Three years later, the large commemorative 9/11 bulletin board still exists and perpetuates the sensationalism of the event.

Other than the problematic bulletin board, 9/11 was not talked about in social studies or other classes. Teachers in my school simply did not teach about it, and this silence allowed racist beliefs and practices to flourish in the school. For example, when students wrapped their T-shirts around their heads and yelled out that they were from India and were terrorists, teachers did not intervene—the students' behavior was merely seen as amusing. On one occasion a social studies teacher joked with students about Muslim names such as Mohammad and Ali. Students in the hallways would often say to South Asian students, "Go back to your country," or "You attacked us." Two students who had been targeted in this way spoke to me about the harassment that was taking place in their daily school experiences. Fellow students had told them to go back to the Middle East and become terrorists. Students would put their arms over their mouths as if to imitate the traditional Muslim headdress (the headdress that covers the entire face but the eyes) as they walked by.

When I spoke to members of the school administration, I was assured that these issues would be investigated with careful scrutiny. I also learned that students had attempted to speak with the guidance counselors at the beginning of the school year, yet months went by and things remained the same. This silence further created an uncomfortable atmosphere that was apparent to me and to those students who were affected. It was unsettling to know that the victimized students had silenced themselves and were dealing with harassment daily. I had to follow up aggressively, and I was only somewhat satisfied with the interventions and the consequences for the students responsible for the harassment. Incidents of racism between Black and White students, for example, were dealt with in a strong manner; school suspensions were given out. But when it came to anti-Arab and anti–South Asian incidents among my students, only after-school detentions were ordered. Taken together, the lack of discussions on the topic and the absence of follow-up on incidents of racial harassment signaled the institutional indifference to this kind of racism.

Given this institutional climate, it was important for me to take ownership of my classroom and initiate a dialogue about these issues, since I believe they should be every teacher's responsibility. This step required risk taking and dealing with possible criticism from parents and school administrators. It was then, in my Spanish-language classroom, that I took the opportunity to engage my students in discussions about their views and assumptions. During a week that was designated annually as World Languages Week, I initiated in-depth discussions with my students about stereotypes, tolerance, and respect. I chose this particular week because it was considered acceptable by school administrators to put aside the regular curriculum and provide students an opportunity to cook food; listen to music; and read about famous figures from French, Italian, and Latino/a cultures. This was my chance to try something new. My curriculum for the week was considered unusual, since teachers have always focused their lessons on Spanish, French, and Italian languages and cultures. My lessons brought in discussions about cultures from South Asia and the Middle East. The goals of my lesson were to engage students in exercises that would require critical and reflective thinking about personal beliefs and viewpoints and, most important, to encourage students to understand the concepts of racial categorization and social justice. For my class, World Languages Week activities consisted of a climate study, paired interviews, large-group discussions, and, finally, a short reflective essay.

During the week prior to World Languages Week, I asked my students to conduct an informal climate study to gain insight into the general atmosphere in the school building. The study provided an informal evaluation of the degree of tolerance and understanding of cultural, social, and religious difference among students. They conducted this informal evaluation through a short questionnaire that I had put together, which contained questions about 9/11 and about racial categories and stereotypes. Each student interviewed two other students in school, outside the class. They asked interviewees to write down their answers on the questionnaires. Students were given a week to gather their data. The questionnaire items included the following:

- Do you feel comfortable telling other students about your background?
- How do students form groups in your school?
- Are these groups related to specific similarities and differences that they share?
- Describe these different groups.

On the 1st day of World Languages Week, students were asked to bring the results of their questionnaires to class. The class sat in a large circle as individual students shared their results. When asking others about the categories "South Asian" and "Muslim," students recorded comments such as "terrorism," "attackers," "turbans," "Al Qaeda," "Taliban," and "Osama bin Laden." In the categories for Latino/a and African American, students recorded more positive comments such as "Spanish speaking" and "Martin Luther King Jr." Over all, the climate study demonstrated that many non-Caucasian students did not share with others at school aspects of their personal backgrounds (i.e., religion and culture). Students also tended to congregate in groupings based on similar racial, ethnic, and socioeconomic background. Racial tensions did indeed already exist in the school, but it was important to note that new stereotypes about the South Asian and Muslim populations emerged and reflected stereotypes that were presented by the media. As a homework assignment, I asked students to reflect on the findings of the climate study that had been shared.

The results of the climate study provided a good basis for a more intimate discussion on these specific stereotypes the following day. For that discussion the students engaged in paired interviews that used questions about each other's backgrounds and their ideas about classifications of people as African American, Latino/a, Asian American, Native American, Arab American, and White. These categories were provided to students on a sheet of paper. Students were to write down what came to mind regarding these racial categorizations. I also wrote the same categories on the chalkboard. Students were asked to write down their responses under the appropriate category on the chalkboard as well. After the paired activity we had a large-group discussion. In all five of my classes, many seventh- and eighth-grade students immediately spoke of Arab Americans as terrorists who wore turbans; were evil; and came from India, Pakistan, and the Middle East. Many students had left the other ethnic categories, such as Latino and African American, listed on the blackboard blank; yet in the space after Arab American I saw the following comments:

- All turbaned men are terrorists.
- All cab drivers in New York City are Osama with their turbans.
- I saw Osama the other day with this long white beard and turban.
- No one should wear turbans in America.
- Everyone over there in the Middle East wants to kill us.
- Osama and All terrorists wear turbans.

Clearly the name Osama was being used as an epithet for terrorism and fear. Students were associating the turban with images of Osama bin Laden that have been sensationalized by the media.

These assumptions about South Asian and Arab Americans spanned socioeconomic differences and the racial divide between Latino, White, and African American students in the classroom and reflected the general attitude in the school building. The statements confirmed that students were not critically evaluating the racist assumptions that were emerging in the wake of 9/11. The atmosphere of the school indirectly supported their feeling that it was acceptable to speak of all those from the East as evil and to assume that stereotypes can be asserted as fact. Students also told me that they had not discussed these issues in any of their other classes. As we approached the end of the 2nd day, I asked them to think about what we had discussed in class and to write a short paragraph for the next day about their own experiences with racism, feeling left out, or being made fun of.

The next day, I spoke to the students about the impact of 9/11 on my own life and worldview. I explained that I had family members who wore turbans and that I myself was from India. I told them about my family's experiences of humiliating searches at airports, about receiving death threats, about being chased through the streets, and about my younger siblings' experiences of harassment in school and being chased off the road while driving. I also brought in newspaper clippings of the various hate crimes, including murders, that had occurred in the United States after 9/11. Hearing what I had to say, students positioned me as the "voice" for Arab Americans and all turbaned men, giving me an opportunity to personalize the discussion and encourage trust building. I then prompted a discussion with students about how stereotypes served to "dehumanize" groups. We discussed how stereotypes are unfair, simplistic generalizations about groups of people that turn them into objects of hatred. This further can lead to a denial of someone's human rights. I then asked them to offer their own experiences and thoughts about racism and stereotypes.

Though the discussion became emotional, I continued with the dialogue. Students began to share very personal details of their experiences with stereotypes and racism. Sharing my personal experiences with students encouraged them to share theirs, and it was a powerful exchange that provided a bridge for understanding. Students spoke about their experiences with racism and their memories of feeling left out. African American students turned the discussion to the racism that they had experienced and the need to educate people about their history. They talked about being judged because of their skin color. Jewish students spoke about the religious discrimination they faced and about family members who were Holocaust survivors. Students shared examples of what was happening in school between different racial groups. In the middle school, students grouped themselves according to their racial background. At the high school, there had been violent outbreaks between the Black and White students, and my students brought these incidents into the conversation as well. There were two South Asian students and one Muslim student in my classes who shared their experiences. The Muslim girl mentioned a house raid that took place at her uncle's house for no apparent reason. The South Asian students spoke about a Sikh parade that took place in Queens, where onlookers threw garbage at the Sikh families.

As we empathized with one another, we became individuals and not stereotypes. It was important for us to hear different viewpoints. It became urgent for us to discuss ineffective and effective ways to deal with conflict.

I then asked students to survey the media that evening and to count the number of times they saw images of Osama bin Laden or the words *fear* and *terror*. I also asked them to look for stereotyped images and language that targeted other groups as well.

The next day, students were eager to talk about what they had seen in the media the night before. They said that they learned about what was really going on. Their comments included the following:

- There were so many images from fighting.
- When I would see pictures of Osama bin Laden, things would race through my mind.
- The terror alert level is always being flashed on the bottom of the screen. It is always saying high or elevated. That makes me scared.
- There were many people always talking about the War on Terror.
- There are frequent images of the twin towers being hit.

Not much to our surprise, students counted 50 or more images of Osama bin Laden, images of other turbaned men, or the words *fear* and *terror* repeated on various channels during a 2-hour period. This was an important observation that further strengthened my emphasis on the role of the media in sensationalizing and generalizing fear.

However, since I also wanted to present positive media images of Sikhs to the students, I ended the week by showing students the movie *Bend It Like Beckham*, which concerns a Sikh family in England and their soccer-playing daughter. There are many moments in the movie where the audience is exposed to music, Sikh traditions, Punjabi clothing, Sikhism, the Punjabi language, and the struggle of immigrant families to balance between two worlds. Students' reactions to the movie ranged from empathy for the characters to a continuing resistance to the turbaned men. Some students enjoyed the music and even danced while others continued to be troubled by images they associated with terrorism. One student asked if the bearded and turbaned men, both the actors and in the framed picture on the wall, were the ayatollah or Osama bin Laden. Others continued to ask why the Sikhs and Osama bin Laden wore the blue-colored turban and said that they looked alike. These moments were opportunities for me to explain to students that the framed picture on the wall was of Guru Nanak Dev, who is considered the god of the Sikhs. I brought in a book from the school library on the Sikhs and passed it around as well.

At the end of World Languages Week, students were asked to write short reflective essays discussing their own reactions to the numerous discussions that we had. Some sample student responses were:

- I think it is nice to know the teacher is from India and that she is very friendly. This helps me be more open to people of different backgrounds.
- It is wrong to judge people. I think if you know someone, like you meet them and get to know them, we can all get along. I think turbans are cool and that even if you wear them it doesn't mean that you are bad or that you are a terrorist. I am glad that we talked about this and I even told my other friend when he called someone Osama that it was wrong.
- We should not judge others so fast. I remember in third grade that I was made fun of because my mom brought food from Mexico and everyone was saying it was gross and they made fun of me for a long time. I felt really bad. I think others probably feel that way too when we make fun of them.
- Things still go through my mind when I see a man in a turban. I get worried if they will hurt me.
- I still am confused; I don't know who the men in turbans are.

The reflective essays were very thoughtful and it was evident that a few students were reevaluating their viewpoints. This was perhaps a small victory. There were students, however, who continued to fear men in turbans or who were resistant to changing their minds. Overall, the most important objectives achieved within a short time span of just 1 week were that the class learned to think critically about stereotypes, built empathy and trust, and developed a healthy criticism of the media and a more complex understanding of world events and people.

CONCLUSION

Discussing controversial issues, according to Diana Hess (2002), correlates with powerful educational outcomes and the effective participation of secondary students in democratic processes. Hess notes that many teachers may not engage in such discussions because of a fear of reprisal. In my experience, speaking about stereotypes and the growing animosity toward targeted groups did spark an emotional discussion in my classroom. But I felt responsible and compelled to engage my students in such dialogues despite the discomfort that I suspected I would feel. I placed myself in a position for the students, where it was acceptable to ask questions and I was approachable.

As I reflected on the value of the lesson within my larger curriculum, I realized that it is important to have such lessons more often and in more classes. I began to share the lessons from my unit and student essays with fellow teachers. I was pleasantly surprised to find that although there was only a handful of interested teachers, we could all try to engage our students in critical thinking activities that deal with issues of social justice. We decided that it was important to strategize and integrate these discussions into our lessons, even though our subjects were generally not seen as a forum for discussing current events. During the following year, I integrated themes of peace building and envisioning peace into my basic curriculum and began to build a small coalition of teachers in the school who shared a similar vision. An Italian teacher (of Italian immigrant background) taught her students to analyze the representation of current events in the media through essays and weekly discussions. An art teacher began to encourage students to depict world events and visions for peace through artistic expression. These are steps in the right direction.

It is important to encourage students to search for facts, challenge their own assumptions, and envision what a peaceful world would look like. Addressing student fears and encouraging students to think about ways to engage in global understanding form important elements of peace pedagogy. Building a vision for peace and encouraging students to be futurists, where they envision a peaceful world, is valuable pedagogy. What is required is teacher initiative to promote discussions on issues of prejudice and stereotyping and to encourage media analysis and awareness of the powerful messages that the media transmit. In this particular case, my perspective as a South Asian created a particular experience for the students. This does not have to be a limitation, however, for other educators. For example, during Black History Month teachers of various backgrounds have been reaching out and providing students an opportunity to learn about the important contributions of African American people. This often becomes a schoolwide celebration as well. Students should, however, be engaged in these types of discussions throughout the year, instead of in isolation. In a similar vein, opening up discussions about the contributions of Asian American, South Asian, Sikh, and Arab American communities is also valuable. These lessons can also be taught by teachers of all backgrounds. Developing a schoolwide commitment to peace and multicultural education would also serve to humanize education, and would provide greater focus on conflict resolution skills, peacemaking, and peer mediation at school.

Resisting elements of "bad sense" in popular culture requires teachers to work against the grain and take a risk as I had to. Numerous Web sites have been developed to provide resources for teachers and parents in order to disseminate knowledge and understanding and to explode myths and stereotypes that are currently being fabricated by the media.

Web sites such as Tolerance.org provide lesson plans for teachers on Sikh immigrants and Arab Americans. Sikheducation.com also provides resources for teachers and stories for students (such as "The Sikh Next Door") and ADC.org has been established to disseminate information and resources about anti–Arab Americanism. Such information helps begin the cycle of understanding and knowledge. Educators for Social Responsibility at Esrnational.org is also rich with resources for educators. I would urge that teaching the student body and staff about issues of respect and compassion should take place at assemblies and in classes. As the pressures for high-stakes testing increase, peace and social justice education is increasingly seen as peripheral. It should be central.

REFERENCES

Hess, D. (2002). Discussing controversial public issues in secondary social studies classrooms: Learning from skilled teachers. *Theory and Research in Social Education, 30*(1), 10–41.

McCarthy, C. (1998). *The uses of culture: Education and the limits of ethnic affiliation.* New York: Routledge.

PART II

Teaching About Globalization

CHAPTER 4

What Is Globalization?

Arthur MacEwan

EVER SINCE Adam and Eve left the Garden, people have been expanding the geographic realm of their economic, political, social, and cultural contacts. In this sense of extending connections to other peoples around the world, globalization is nothing new. Also, as a process of change that can embody both great opportunities for wealth and progress and great trauma and suffering, globalization at the beginning of the 21st century is following a well-established historical path. Yet the current period of change in the international system does have its own distinctive features, not the least important of which is the particular sort of political conflict it is generating.

"GREATEST EVENTS" AND "DREADFUL MISFORTUNES"

We are fond of viewing our own period as one in which great transformations are taking place, and it is easy to recite a list of technological and social changes that have dramatically altered the way we live and the way we connect to peoples elsewhere in the world. Yet other surges of globalization in the modern era have been similarly disruptive to established practices. The first surge by which we might mark the beginning of modern globalization came with the invasion of the Western Hemisphere by European powers and with their extension of ocean trade around Africa to Asia. Adam Smith, writing *The Wealth of Nations* in 1776, did not miss the significance of these developments:

> The discovery of America, and that of a passage to the East Indies by the Cape of Good Hope, are the two greatest and most important events recorded in the history of mankind. . . . By uniting, in some measure, the most distant parts of the world, by enabling them to relieve one another's wants, to

increase one another's enjoyments, and to encourage one another's industry, their general tendency would seem to be beneficial. (Smith, 1776/1852,
p. 258)

Alongside what Adam Smith saw as the great gains of globalization
(not his term!), were the slaughter, through battle and disease, of millions
of Native Americans, the enslavement and associated deaths of millions
of Africans, and the subjugation of peoples in Asia. Smith did recognize
the "dreadful misfortunes" that fell upon the peoples of the East and West
Indies as a result of these "greatest . . . events" (though he does not men-
tion Africans in this expression of concern). He saw these misfortunes,
however, as arising "rather from accident than from any thing in the nature of the events themselves" (pp. 258–259).

The first stage of modern globalization illustrates not only the combined great gains and "dreadful misfortunes" that have characterized globalization but also the vast scope of the process. The political and economic
changes that followed from the European conquest of the Americas and
forays into Asia are relatively well known. Equally momentous were the
huge cultural transformations that were tied to the great expansion of
economic contacts among the continents. Peoples moved, or they were
moved by force. As they came to new locations and in contact with other
peoples, almost every aspect of their lives was altered—from what people
eat ("Italian" spaghetti comes from Asia and the tomatoes for the sauce
from America) to their music (jazz is now the best-known example, blend-
ing the backgrounds of different continents to emerge in America) to religion (the cross accompanied the sword in the era of colonial conquest).

The second great surge of modern globalization came in the 19th century, both as product and cause of the Industrial Revolution. On the one
hand, the expansion of industry generated large reductions in transport
costs that brought huge increases in international commerce. On the other
hand, for the emerging commercial centers of Europe and North America,
the opening of foreign markets and access to foreign sources of raw materials fueled (sometimes literally) the expansion of industry. Great Britain,
as the "workshop of the world," was at the center of these changes and
over the course of the century saw its foreign trade increase three times
as rapidly as national income.

Britain during the 19th century provided a foreshadowing of current-
day globalization as it officially touted "free trade" as the proper mode of
organization for commerce—not just for itself, but for the entire world.
The gospel of "free trade" was then carried around the globe by the British navy, and heroic ideological gymnastics allowed a growing colonial
empire to be included under this same rubric. As the British historian E. J.

Hobsbawm has commented, "British industry could grow up, by and large, in a protected home market until strong enough to demand free entry into other people's markets, that is 'Free Trade'." In today's globalization it is the United States, a country that also attained its economic power on the foundation of protectionism, that preaches the gospel of "free trade" to the rest of the world.

Present-day globalization is, by and large, a continuation of the process that began in the 19th century (which in turn had its roots in the great transformation that began along with the 16th century). Two world wars and the Great Depression disrupted the progress of globalization for some 60 years and shifted its center from Britain to the United States, but it is now back on track. By the 1980s, the extent of economic connections that had been established among the world's national economies by 1913 had been reattained, and in subsequent years international trade and investment have continued to expand their roles in the economies of most nations.[1]

HOMOGENIZATION AND COMPETITION

Change in the world economy today, however, is not simply an extension of what went on in earlier periods, not simply a quantitative extension of well-established trends. What distinguishes the current era from earlier phases of globalization is that now capitalism is ubiquitous. Virtually everywhere, production takes place for profit and is based on wage labor. In the 19th century, capitalism may have provided the leading dynamic of the international economy, but in many parts of the world—most everywhere outside Europe and North America—a great deal of economic activity was organized through families (peasant farms or shops), under semifeudal conditions, or through slavery. These activities were all connected to markets and to a world capitalist system, but they were not capitalist in themselves. Certainly there are important aspects of life and work today that take place outside markets and are not directly capitalist—for example, work in the home, interactions within governments, volunteer activity, and some other forms of production. Yet capitalism holds sway, dominating and defining economic relationships in almost all parts of the world.

The ubiquity of capitalism gives a new character to the economic connections among peoples in distant parts of the world. There has, in particular, been a grand homogenization, both of consumer markets and of production activity. Wal-Mart and McDonald's establish themselves in Mexico to sell the same sorts of products in the same way as in the United States. At the same time, Mexican workers at the Ford plant in Hermosillo produce the same cars that are produced in U.S. factories and they do so with equipment and procedures that are among the most "modern" in the world. Also on the production side, plants in Mexico and the United States are sometimes integrated with one another in a "global assembly line," with Mexican workers engaged in the labor-intensive aspects of the operation and U.S. workers engaged in the more highly skilled activities; for example, in clothing production, design and cutting is done in the United States while the pieces are stitched together on the Mexican side of the border.

Mexico, because of its proximity to the United States and the reduction of trade restrictions between the two countries, presents an extreme example of the cross-border integration of production. Yet in broad terms, we are presented today with a new international organization of production, as people in different corners of the globe produce the same sorts of products with the same technologies and often for the same employers—though the ultimate employers often operate through local subcontractors.

The homogenization of the world economy creates a new set of relationships, a direct competition, among workers in different parts of the world. Although such competition always existed, it is much more extensive and intense than in the past and, most important, it takes place between workers whose wages are dramatically different from each other's. It is one thing when U.S. and Canadian workers, who have very similar wages and standards of living, are in competition with each other. It is quite another thing when the U.S. and Canadian workers are in competition with Mexican workers.

This new relationship among workers in different countries presents obvious problems for workers in the rich countries: They simply cannot compete with workers who, using the same equipment and methods of production (i.e., the same technology), are paid far, far lower wages. Yet similar, though perhaps less obvious, problems exist for the low-wage workers. With wage labor markets existing throughout most of the world, virtually all workers are placed in competition with one another. While workers in Bangladesh may be willing to accept very low wages to assemble clothing for the European market, they are always faced with the prospect that Vietnamese workers may accept even lower wages. Or Indonesian workers, who assemble sports shoes for the U.S. market, may face the prospect of production innovations that will substitute machinery and skilled workers for unskilled workers on an assembly line, making it profitable for the firms to move their production back to the United States.

In a capitalist world, where many different sites around the globe provide firms with the labor markets they need, those firms can have a great advantage over workers. That advantage, however, depends upon "free trade," the elimination of government barriers to the movement of goods and funds across national boundaries. Free trade has given firms the option of either moving themselves or moving their sources of supply in response to cost differences (wage differences, but also other cost differences). Free trade, however, does not include the reduction—let alone the elimination—of barriers to the movement of workers. So labor does not enjoy the same freedom in the globalized economy as that enjoyed by capital. Since "freedom" means having alternatives, and having alternatives means having power, a system that enhances the freedom of firms relative to the freedom of labor means giving businesses more power relative to labor. (Even were barriers to migration to be reduced, there would still be substantial costs to labor movement compared with that of capital movement; and capital's advantage, while reduced, would not be eliminated.)

The drive for free trade existed, as pointed out above, in the British-led globalization of the 19th century, but the United States has been able to push the concept to a whole new level. In part, free trade is important for the power it confers on business, but it is also important as ideology. The ideology of free trade has provided the defining rationale for the North American Free Trade Agreement (NAFTA), the Free Trade Agreement of the Americas (FTAA), the World Trade Organization (WTO), and the programs pushed on low-income countries by the International Monetary Fund (IMF) and the World Bank. The opening of markets, the opening of sources of supply, the spread of private economic activity—all this is supposed to provide a new era of rapid economic growth for the world and serve the needs of the poor as well as the rich.

NOT SO FAST

The concept of free trade has a certain intuitive appeal. After all, if the firms and people of a nation are free to buy their supplies from the lowest-cost source of supply, then they will be able to buy more and satisfy their needs more thoroughly than if their government limits the sources from which they can buy those supplies (bans imports) or imposes extra costs (tariffs) on supplies from abroad. For low-income countries, desperate for economic growth, it would seem absurd for their governments to place restrictions on imports, forcing firms and people to waste resources on expensive domestic goods. Moreover, it only takes a moment's reflection to note the huge gains we realize from international commerce: not only the banana I eat for breakfast and a good portion of the oil that fuels my car and heats my home, but also the ideas and culture from elsewhere in the world—to say nothing of the competitive pressures from abroad that help drive economic advances in my own country. For a small country, the gains from foreign commerce are a virtual necessity.

Another moment's reflection, however, reveals that things are not so simple. Free trade is not the only way to engage extensively in international commerce. In fact, none of the countries we now denote as "developed" attained their development through free trade, though all engaged extensively in international commerce. There are, it seems, some substantial advantages to having the production of certain kinds of goods take place within a country, as compared with obtaining those same goods from abroad. The U.S. textile industry in the 19th century, the U.S. auto industry through most of the 20th century, the Japanese computer industry in the mid-20th century, the South Korean steel and shipbuilding industries later in the 20th century—all generated broad economic gains in terms of the transformation of technology and the formation of a skilled work force that far surpassed the costs that arose from the government protection they received in their early stages of expansion. None of this provides a justification for protectionism in general; continuing protection of sugar and steel production in the United States imposes costs with no offsetting benefits (except to those directly engaged in the industries). Yet the experience of 2 centuries of capitalist development does demonstrate the fallacy of the free trade argument. Efforts by the U.S. government to push free trade on low-income countries today may make sense from the perspective of the interests of U.S. firms, but it is hardly a prescription for economic advancement in low-income countries.

But there is more. Globalization as it is being organized under the banner of free trade is doing nothing to reduce the "development gap," the huge difference in material well-being between the peoples of the rich nations and the peoples of most of the rest of the world. In fact, there is some evidence that under the regime of increasingly open world markets, the development gap is increasing. Worse yet: There is a good deal of evidence that free trade globalization is contributing to increasing inequality within nations, not only within the low-income countries of the "South" but also within the United States and the other high-income countries of the "North."

As the international economy is increasingly organized in a way that enhances the power of firms and tends to undermine the power of labor, it is certainly likely that greater inequality will be the outcome. Unfortunately, available data do not allow us to draw strong conclusions about what has been happening to world income inequality in recent decades. What we do know is that income distribution in today's world is already grossly unequal, with hundreds of millions of people living at the edge of subsistence, while the elites in all countries live in obscene luxury. We also know that, although some low-income countries have made substantial gains (for example, South Korea and some other countries of East Asia), the current surge of globalization has provided no general relief for the world's poor. Furthermore, we know that globalization—new patterns of international trade and investment—has disrupted people's lives, pushed people out of their traditional lines of work, shifted the location of economic activity, and forced people to adopt new patterns of consumption. All this makes many people's lives very unpleasant, regardless of what can be uncovered with the aggregate statistics regarding income distribution and economic growth.

WHAT ELSE IS NEW?

One might well absorb this summary of change in the world economy and respond with the comment: So, what else is new? It does seem that periods of great change in the world economy, whatever immediate benefits they may generate for the elite and whatever their long-run benefits for society in general, are accompanied by severe disruptions, hardships, and inequalities. Current experience seems to fit well with the pattern established in the 16th and 19th centuries, to say nothing of earlier eras of imperial expansion. (Many commentators quite reasonably reject the term *globalization* in favor of *imperialism* precisely because the latter term underscores the great inequalities of power and income that are always so important in international affairs.)

Yet perhaps there is something new in the current era in the particular type of political response to globalization that has been generated in recent years. The "dreadful misfortunes" of earlier eras have also generated political responses—sometimes in the form of spontaneous rebellion, sometimes as more organized resistance and revolution, and sometimes as waves of new oppositional organizations and alliances. The political response to globalization at the beginning of the 21st century, however, has some distinguishing characteristics that are worth emphasizing.

Most important, parts of the response to globalization are themselves global. The "coming-out party" for the antiglobalization movement in Seattle in the fall of 1999 involved people and organizations from all over the world. As a coordinated effort by groups from many rich countries and many poor countries, the action in Seattle—and the ones that have followed in Washington, Quebec, Prague, Pôrto Alegre, and elsewhere— suggest that something is different about the nature of political action. Many times, opposition movements based on national identities have, at least implicitly, been in conflict with one another; at other times, organizations in rich countries have opted to "support" groups in poor countries, but not as a joint and coordinated effort. While progressive movements have always talked about their internationalism, this time around the talk may translate more effectively into practice.

Also, the globalization of political opposition to globalization has included steps by labor unions, which have long adhered to highly nationalist positions. So far, more of the new internationalism of the U.S. labor movement has been in the realm of rhetoric rather than practice, but U.S. unions have made some important efforts at cross-border organizing—in the form, for example, of supporting efforts of Mexican workers to organize firms in their country that supply the U.S. market. (NAFTA, while allowing corporations, the organizations of capital, to operate in both the United States and Mexico, as well as in Canada, makes no parallel provision for unions, the organizations of labor.) The rhetoric of internationalism, too, is important, especially because it marks such a departure from the past practices of the U.S. labor movement. Some critics complain that the newfound interest of the U.S. labor movement in conditions abroad arises from its own immediate concerns, the competition from low-cost imports, instead of from a concern for workers elsewhere in the world. But that is just the point. If globalization forces U.S. unions to secure the interests of their own members by pursuing a new internationalism, then that is certainly a significant change.

The organized opposition to globalization goes far beyond the labor movement, however, involving a wide spectrum of social movements. Environmental and women's organizations, peasant groupings, student-based action committees, and others have all been a part of the actions. In addition, well-established nongovernmental organizations such as Oxfam, while not engaged in the protest actions in Seattle and elsewhere, have been a part of the general opposition to globalization. Not only is this opposition based on a wide range of social movements, but these different movements have at least begun to work in alliance with one another. Some aspects of this alliance, particularly that between environmental groups and labor unions, suggest a major shift from past conflicts.

Opposition actions have taken place in a wide spectrum of countries. On the one hand, there have been the much publicized actions led by young, often middle-class activists in the United States, focused on meetings of the principal international economic agencies such as the IMF, World Bank, and WTO. On the other hand, there have been actions in India, where peasant organizations have demonstrated against the international pharmaceutical and seed companies that are trying to use the internationalization of patent regulations to secure control of world markets. While these geographically disparate actions are not coordinated through any cohesive international organization, they are part of an interconnected movement.

The opposition to globalization that has developed is not a cohesive movement, and it is not so well developed that we can have confidence in its lasting impact. Furthermore, it has many problems. Opposition to globalization sometimes is expressed as an opposition to connections with other peoples rather than as an opposition to the way those connections are exacerbating inequalities of power and income. Thus xenophobic protectionism is sometimes just below the surface of protest actions. By and large, however, the opposition to globalization appears to be based on an internationalism that may provide a foundation for a progressive, and perhaps lasting, movement.

The more serious problems of this opposition arise from the difficulties in coming to grips with the power and complexity of the globalization process itself. A small example is provided by efforts in the rich countries to respond to the proliferation of imports of goods produced in "sweatshop" conditions in low-income countries. Protests against the companies that use these shops—firms such as Nike and Gap—are met with the response that workers in these factories are eager to obtain their jobs because these jobs are significantly better in terms of pay and working conditions than other available jobs. What's more, the response is often true. A sophisticated movement can come to terms with this reality by emphasizing the need to alter the context that impoverishes workers in low-income countries and by stressing that such a context is most effectively transformed through political struggle. Also, by focusing on workers' right to political freedom—in particular, the right to organize unions—rather than on particular aspects of workers' conditions, antisweatshop activists can have a positive impact.

The "sweatshop" example helps clarify that globalization is not simply a collection of practices, not simply a peculiar set of connections between peoples around the globe. It is part of the long historical development and spread of capitalism. Within the framework of capitalism, it is difficult to solve problems that are based on the inequality of income and power, because those problems are generated by the system itself. Nonetheless, capitalism is not an immutable system, and it is probably not a permanent one. The oppositional struggles are not only responses to globalization; they are part of the process of globalization itself. They will play a role in shaping events and in influencing the entire nature of the process. And they will contribute to answering the question, What is globalization?

NOTE

1. We usually measure the extent of economic connections by levels of imports and exports relative to total production or by the level of international investment relative to total production. For example, in 1913, U.S. exports were 6% as large as gross domestic product (GDP); the figure had fallen to 4.6% in 1950, but was up to 7.1% in 1973 and 10.6% in 1999. For Europe, the figures are 22% in 1913, 16.7% in 1950, 21.8% in 1973, and 32.1% in 1999. Interestingly, Japan, for which exports were 20% of GDP in 1913, saw this figure remain relatively stable at around 10% of GDP in the second half of the 20th century. Figures on foreign investment are harder to come by for the early part of the 20th century, but they seem to show a similar pattern. In recent years, the foreign investment figures show strong increases of economic connections. In the 1985–1990 period, for the world as a whole, foreign direct investments (i.e., not including financial investments) were 5.4% of the level of GDP in the countries making the investments and 6% of GDP in the countries receiving the investments; in the 1996–1998 period, the figures had risen to 8.2% and 8.4%, respectively.

REFERENCE

Smith, A. *Inquiry into the nature and causes of the wealth of nations.* London: Nelson, 1852. (Original work published 1776)

CHAPTER 5

Sweating the Small Stuff:
Mickey, Michael, and the Global Sweatshop

Maria Sweeney with Marjorie Feld

FOR THE PAST 12 years, I have been teaching elementary school in a predominantly White, upper-middle-class elementary public school in New Jersey. I use a whole-language approach, which means that my fourth-grade students develop their skills and strategies as readers through reading whole texts they have chosen. Writing on topics they have also chosen, and writing for a real audience, they develop writing skills and strategies. For each of my chosen themes in the year's social studies curriculum—all related to issues of social justice—the students put together research questions and then create an open-ended inquiry project.

Every year, as school begins to wind down at the beginning of May, I ask my students to choose one topic for an end-of-the-year play to be performed for our entire school, kindergarten through Grade 5. I require that their topic be of social significance, concerning an issue they care about and want others to learn about. In past years, students have chosen to research and write plays on the Montgomery bus boycott, the "truth" about Columbus, the Paterson silk strike of 1913, and the South African elections.

Three years ago, students in my class chose the global sweatshop as the topic of their play. When we discussed possible companies on which to focus our inquiry, Nike was at the top of the list. "Most kids think they can't live without Nike," one student observed. The others agreed that the company holds great sway over young people. Several wondered if we could even compete with its power: "The whole point of the play would be to get them to join the boycott," one student cautioned, "but most kids would never stop wearing Nike stuff. It wouldn't be cool at all to be against Nike." Despite these misgivings, they concluded that Nike needed to be researched because "kids should know all the horrible things they are doing." Aware that Nike has been a leader in corporate exploitation of Third

World low-wage labor, and that a wealth of information was available about its crimes, I strongly endorsed their choice.

Choosing a second company was equally straightforward. During an earlier discussion on current events, I shared material prepared by the National Labor Committee about the inhumane treatment of workers in Disney plants in Haiti. One student suggested that we focus on Disney to reach the younger kids in the audience, because Nike products are worn more often by those in the upper grades. Someone else called our attention to a statement from a recent Disney annual report posted on our current events bulletin board: "Today, children around the world go to bed holding Mickey Mouse dolls, and Mickey's likeness appears on clothing, books, and products in lands around the globe. Disney lives in the hearts, memories, and minds of people everywhere." Pointing to the statement, the student said, "That's why we have to tell them about Disney, too."

We began the project with 4 weeks of research on the problem of multinational corporations' exploitation of Third World labor, discussing especially the concepts of economic globalization and capital's drive to find cheap labor in order to drive up profits. These were complex concepts for 9- and 10-year-olds, but they became accessible through careful presentation. From an earlier labor history unit, my students had gotten a mental framework within which to understand workers' struggles. During the course of that unit, in which we studied a locally important strike, Paterson's silk strike of 1913, students became convinced of the necessity for unions in a capitalist economy. There they also encountered many of the same themes they studied in the global-sweatshop unit. In Paterson, we learned, the silk mill owners moved their operations to the anthracite region of Pennsylvania, where they found a cheap, isolated, and unorganized source of labor in the wives of coal miners. The students often drew analogies between the mill owners earlier in the century and modern-day Nike and Disney labor practices.

Working with partners, the children read materials from the Nike boycott home page and the National Labor Committee's report on Disney; they drafted charts in their notebooks listing key components of the problems. We then synthesized their notes into a class chart that included the following points: Pay is not enough to live on; workers are forced to work like crazy to meet quotas; they are harassed by bosses; they lack health insurance and other benefits; they are punished if they try to form unions. I also defined basic vocabulary, such as *subcontracting, minimum wage* versus *liveable wage, benefits, exploitation, quotas,* and *independent monitoring.* In the future—Bill Bigelow (1997) suggests this—I will supplement these introductory readings with some exercises that would help the students view the problem of global sweatshops as part of global capitalism and not just the work of a few unscrupulous companies.

Following this general introduction, students embarked on scavenger hunts at home: They were to bring in all the Nike and Disney products they owned in order to see the way the global sweatshop affected their own lives. When a few students discovered that they didn't own any Nike or Disney products, they asked whether they could gather other companies' household items made in the Third World. When the children returned, they carried bags of athletic clothes, pajamas, sneakers, and toys. We again made a class chart, categorizing the various types of items, companies, and countries of origin.

The students were amazed to discover that almost nothing was made in the United States. I then shared with them the story of a garment company in the news a few years before. The company moved from Michigan, where seamstresses earned $7–8 an hour, to Haiti, where the workers' hourly wage was 30¢. One child in the class, who served as devil's advocate with lots of verbal ammunition brought from home, proclaimed that companies have the right to move if they can "make their stuff cheaper someplace else." Another student reminded him of the information recorded on our original chart, which contrasted the earnings of Nike's and Disney's chiefs (Phil Knight and Michael Eisner, respectively) with the meager wages of their workers. I also reminded the children that in addition to CEOs' gaining enormous earnings, shareholders reaped great profits. I referred them to a statistic we had noted earlier: Michael Jordan's earnings for 1 year of Nike endorsements ($20 million) is equal to the combined pay of 120,000 Indonesians working in Nike plants. "Michael Eisner is like a vacuum cleaner," said one student. "He sucks everything out of the workers and gives them just barely enough to survive."

Since all our materials, both video and print, were designed for adult audiences and consequently were quite dense, I frequently needed to explain their content. Each child had a folder and a learning log for organizing materials, taking notes, and writing reflections. I scheduled several long blocks of time for research, viewing videos, discussion, and writing. Typically, at the beginning of each research period, I introduced a new resource, defined vocabulary, and outlined the major points in the material. I wrote this up on chart paper for the children's reference. I opened the study of each company with a video: *Mickey Mouse Goes to Haiti* on Disney and the CBS *48 Hours* segment "Nike in Vietnam." While both videos proved excellent introductions to the conditions of workers' lives, I frequently had to pause the tapes in order to answer questions and clarify situations. After viewing the videos, the children wrote notes as well as quite moving personal responses.

They studied the print materials, taken mostly from the National Labor Committee report and the Web pages, with partners or in small groups. Finally, we collectively wrote the fact sheets detailing key problems (wage disparities), important statistics (the workers' mortality rates), and anecdotes (the prohibition on workers' talking, for example) about each company. We kept adding to these sheets as we obtained significant information.

It was at this point, however, that I realized that the children had gained a wealth of knowledge without sensing the humanity of the workers whose cause they supported, and whom they would later represent in the play. To stimulate an emotional connection, I assigned the class to do presentations that were to be both written and visual portraits of workers. We read passages describing the lives of several workers in Haiti and Indonesia. I read aloud and had the students close their eyes and "become" the person whose life I read about. We viewed the videos again, this time trying to see and "know" each individual caught in the camera's frame. Then we examined photos of workers and their surroundings. The students' poems, letters, and stories, written from the point of view of workers, were to capture individual lives using strong images and details. Most of their portraits were quite realistic and moving.

This activity shifted the tone in the classroom, as it authentically engaged the students' sense of the needless human misery caused by the global sweatshop. However, though they spoke of the workers with greater compassion, they presented portraits of workers as both hopeless and helpless, aware of inequity but unable to address it. Fortunately, the former Indonesian Nike worker Cicih Sukaesih was at that time touring the Americas. This young woman's story offered my students a heartening example of one worker, among many, fighting for justice. She and 23 coworkers were fired for organizing the walkout of 6,200 employees, and she was now in the United States to meet with Phil Knight and demand back wages and the rehiring of the fired workers. On the Web page of the organization Global Exchange, we read Sukaesih's speeches, in which she told of the intolerable, abusive conditions in Nike plants and urged independent monitoring of factories. The students now saw that many Third World workers were seriously involved in a movement against sweatshop conditions, though unfortunately they did not breathe life into these images in their play.

When a parent complained that our work was only presenting "one side of the story," I knew another, final exercise was needed. (Each year, to sense the extent to which I can pursue a social justice curriculum, I must assess the politics of my students' parents, a cautionary measure I will discuss below.) The unit Perspectives and Interests was designed to help the students think critically about the perspectives and interests behind each resource we used, including new materials I obtained from the public relations departments of Nike and Disney. Integrating these documents into our lesson marked my attempt to incorporate the companies' side.

Inquiring into the motivations behind each source, we soon decided that those who lobbied for the rights of Nike and Disney workers, such as the National Labor Committee and the organization Press for Change, were not driven by selfish interests and were not getting rich from their work. The public relations documents, however, drew harsh criticism from the students. One denial of abusive practices in overseas plants was accompanied by claims that workers enjoyed gardens and basketball courts, to which one student replied: "If there really is a basketball court, big deal. They're cheap to build and the workers probably never have time to play anyway, since they have to work so many hours." Citing the interviews and writings as evidence, the children also insisted that the companies had lied when refuting reports of abusive working conditions and starvation wages.

We discussed the goal of any company's public relations department: to promote a positive public image and thereby enhance earnings. In contrast to motives of the human rights groups, driven by morality or a desire for justice, the corporate motive was profits. During this exercise we also analyzed the perspectives of opinion and editorial pieces, letters to the editor, "objective" news articles, and Internet items. Who were the authors of each piece, and what might they gain by convincing us that their point is the right one? Asking such questions was only a modest introduction to critical reading of resources, but it helped to demystify the slick documents produced by public relations departments. The exercise assured us, and the students' parents, that we had considered a range of views.

Finally, after 4 weeks of research on the global sweatshop, the students began the playwriting process. For a few nights, their homework was to write up ideas for the play on their own. In class they reviewed our fact sheets, worked in groups brainstorming about possible scenes, and drew ideas from every member of the class. Together we decided on the play's framework and a list of eight scenes. The students signed up for the scene in which they wanted to act, thereby committing themselves to writing their own lines. Each scene's writing group received the documents relevant to its subject. Every afternoon for a week the groups wrote, acted, and revised their scenes. The entire class viewed each group's scenes and provided feedback. By the end we had gone over every aspect of the script several times. While the process proved tedious at times, it was worth the effort to have the entire class agree upon what we would present.

After grappling with this complex and disturbing information during those first 4 weeks, the students crafted a cohesive, inspiring, and intelligent piece of writing. The script was impressive and hard hitting. The students began with the familiar scenes taking place on our school playground at recess and at a local McDonalds, and then had the audience travel to Nike and Disney factories and after that to Michael Jordan's mansion and to the corporate offices of the two companies. Throughout, they represented their own political education: they showed other kids learning the meaning of the word *exploit* and connecting it to their own purchases; they offered a window through which to view a struggling, hungry family in Haiti; they demonstrated the apathy of Jordan and Eisner (Eisner was, by the way, counting his millions when first encountered). The play ends on a note of hope, as two students discuss the growing union movements in the Third World and then present themselves as active agents of change in the same movement: "If we can get tons of people to join in this movement," one actor says, "I think we can make a difference." The play concludes with the other actor's response: "So what are we waiting for? Let's get started." It was clear to me that the students truly believed in the message they wanted to communicate.

That message, however, was stopped before it could be received by anyone. Three days before the performance for the entire school, my principal entered the classroom and told me that the material was inappropriate for the intended audience: the children wouldn't understand the play and the younger students might be upset by it. She also asserted that my students could not have possibly understood an issue as complex as the global sweatshop, as evidenced by the one-sided nature of the script. The performance would be for only the parents.

When I announced this decision, one student cried, "That's censorship!" The others agreed. I felt unprepared for their strong response: They were angry and incredulous, and a few even cried. They insisted on writing letters to the administration to plead their case. These brilliant letters made a strong case for the play. One student wrote that "we know more than you think"; another accused the administration of ageism. But these letters, like those they wrote to Michael Jordan, went unanswered.

What happened next was pure luck. The day of the play, Jeff Ballinger, the founder of Press for Change, was surprised to discover that the play was to be performed for parents only. He contacted the *New York Times*, and the article the newspaper ran attracted attention from people and media all over the country. Letters of protest poured into the school. Scott Ellis, the resident director of a Broadway theater, saw the article and offered his theater for a performance in October 1996. Our play was to open on Broadway (Karp, 1997/1998).

While I continued to be interviewed by the national media throughout the summer, most of the coverage focused on the kids' Broadway performance rather than the play's central issues concerning social justice. School officials, meanwhile, reiterated their objections to the play's being seen by their younger students, but praised the opportunity for students to work with theater professionals.

From the refusal of the administration in June through our performance in October, always present in my mind was that my teaching in a privileged district was underpinning the entire endeavor. We had plentiful resources in order to put the show together. Many stay-at-home mothers offered their big vans, donated props, and ran phone chains for communication. One parent, who takes photographs for a national magazine, donated head shots of each student to display in the theater lobby. Another parent used her connections to obtain a loan, and with that money we made videos of the play that people could purchase. The contradictions of upper-middle-class privilege allowed us to reach the high level we did.

On a broader and more personal level, several elements contributed to our success. The positive rapport I have with my superintendent certainly allowed us to make the most of the opportunities offered to us, and may have in fact prevented me from losing my job. I also think that maintaining professionalism was then and remains today absolutely necessary in order to be true to the way I want to teach. Every year, I measure the political climate in which I am working, because I know that to ignore this would be reckless; I would risk my job and thus the opportunity to make progressive change.

I must always respond to claims that I am showing "one side of the story" by carefully and seriously documenting a legitimate defense. As I noted above, when a parent claimed "bias" in the process of our Nike/Disney play research, I distributed documents from the two companies and reconstructed the entire history of how the script was written. On this and other similar occasions, I emphasize that my students approach issues from multiple perspectives and try to view those perspectives critically. Teaching from a social justice and critical literacy perspective necessitates that I locate a balance between risk taking and pushing the limits of my work environment in order to retain my job for future years of transformative reaching.

The story of this particular event in my teaching career became extraordinary only after the decision to ban it from our school audience; until that point, it was an ordinary year, when students once again created a play that took my breath away. Children have tremendous ethical and intellectual capabilities, usually left untapped and undeveloped. While as a teacher of social justice I have had to be unpopular more than once, the immense satisfaction I gain from watching students come to political consciousness cannot be overstated.

REFERENCES

Bigelow, B. (1997, Summer). The human lives behind the labels: The global sweatshop, Nike, and the race to the bottom. *Rethinking Schools, 11*(4), 1–5.

Karp, S. (1997/1998, Winter). Banned in New Jersey, welcomed on Broadway. *Rethinking Schools, 12*(2), 14–15.

Planting Seeds of Solidarity

Bob Peterson

MY FIFTH-GRADE students love stories. Almost every day after lunch I light a candle, turn off the lights, and read or tell a story. If something interferes with story time, I receive a chorus of complaints.

One of the stories I use to start my students' study of globalization issues is from my own teenage experience when I lived in Cairo, Egypt, in the mid 1960s. I tell my students that I lived in Cairo among pyramids and sphinxes, close to the world's longest river, the Nile. I attended a middle school with kids from all over the world, in an old palace of former king of Egypt Farouk. Because my family was from the United States and my father had a good job as a soil scientist, we lived comfortably in a suburban home south of Cairo. I had many adventures—riding horses and camels by the Great Pyramids of Cheops, visiting Tutankhamen's tomb in the Valley of the Kings, swimming in the Red Sea—but one incident stands out in my memory.

One sunny afternoon my family got into our blue 1965 Ford station wagon and drove 20 kilometers south of Cairo to climb a lesser-known pyramid called the Red Pyramid. My mother had packed a lunch in our cooler, including some cans of imported diet soda for my diabetic brother, Don. We picnicked in an isolated spot in the desert a ways from the Red Pyramid. By the time we finished, a small group of children had gathered around our car, and they called out in Arabic, "Baksheesh! baksheesh!" They wanted a tip—money. Their little hands poked through the open car windows, begging.

We did not give money to the kids (U.S. tourists were "not encouraged" to do so)—but we did "give" them something. As we were leaving we threw out the window my brother's two empty aluminum cans. "They want them for a toy," my father said as we drove away. The children screamed with joy. I looked out the back window as we slowly drove toward the pyramid. The children were piled on top of the cans, fighting to be owner of their newly found playthings.

We hiked to the top of the pyramid's peak, but my thoughts remained focused on the children fighting over what I had thrown away. Why was I destined to be the one in the car tossing junk to poor kids, instead of the one who was begging for a penny or an empty can?

WHY?

Using simple stories to raise profound questions is among the oldest and best of teaching techniques. It is also an essential strategy in my teaching about globalization issues.

I view teaching about globalization and world justice issues much as I view issues of multicultural education. They need to be both woven throughout the curriculum and highlighted in specific lessons. This approach is necessary in part to find the time to teach about the issues, given all that elementary teachers are expected to cover. But also I find that an integrated approach helps motivate students and teaches them that these are central issues that cannot be dealt with in one or two activities. As a result, my lessons in math, science, social studies, writing, reading, current events—even discipline discussions—all have a world justice and multicultural theme woven throughout.

Teaching about global issues is not the norm in U.S. classrooms and I have struggled with how best to approach the topic. One of the dilemmas I have encountered is that I don't want to negate my students' instinctive feelings of empathy and caring, yet I want them to move beyond what in this country is often an "us versus them" dichotomy. I have found that discussions of globalization can feed into the inherently condescending attitude that people in the United States have all the answers, that people in "developing" countries are somehow inferior or less than human, and that the role of those in the United States is to "help the less fortunate."

In this chapter, I focus on activities that attempt to move beyond the "us versus them" dichotomy and instead engender feelings of solidarity with others around the world. This by no means encompasses my teaching about globalization and there are other important issues, such as how I approach colonialism, world economics, environmental concerns, social activism, and building solidarity and community within my own classroom. (For a fuller discussion of these issues, see Bigelow & Peterson, 2002).

The story of my year in Egypt provokes thoughtful comments and questions among students. They express surprise that some children have so little and they wonder what life is like for children around the world. "I can't believe kids actually wanted just an old can," I recall a student saying. A response from another student stressed our commonalty: "I believe it. Every kid wants to play!"

PROBLEM-POSING APPROACH

Throughout my classroom discussions on globalization, I pose more questions, not so much in search of a specific answer, but for all of us to think about: How are our lives different from theirs? How are they similar? What do people in this country have to learn from people in other countries? Why does chance allow for some to live a life of relative luxury while others don't know where their next meal is coming from? And what might we do about such things?

There's no doubt that global problems are complex. However, even with elementary children there is no reason to unnecessarily simplify things. Questioning or problem posing is an effective means to keep discussions both interesting and complicated.

Early in the year, I use Tracy Chapman's song "Why?" to pose questions. Chapman asks, for example, "Why do the babies starve when there is enough food to feed the world?" I give my students a copy of the lyrics (as I do with dozens of songs and poems we use in the classroom) to keep in a special three-ring binder, so that they might refer to them throughout the year. Needless to say, we don't answer Chapman's question of "Why?" We note it, sometimes adding it to the spiral notebook hanging on the wall titled "Questions We Have." I ask students what they think might be answers to her question and we note them as well. Ideas usually include a range of possibilities: lack of food, no jobs, too many people, war, drugs, and lazy people. I tell my students that this is but one example of the important questions we will ponder in fifth grade.

In the beginning weeks, I also share a few basic statistics from UNICEF, including the fact that about 30,000 children die daily from malnutrition and preventable illness. I ask my class, "How many schools with the same student population as ours would it take to equal the number of children who die each day?" This helps make the large number meaningful, and it usually surprises the students at the depth of the problem. I also might share statistics, such as approximately 130 million children do not attend elementary school, 1.1 billion people have no access to safe drinking water, and 3 billion lack adequate sanitation facilities.

I tell the students that we are going to try to not just feel sorry for or sympathize with those people, but to develop "solidarity." I have a student look up the word *solidarity* in the dictionary, and they find that it means "unity, based on a community of interests." We discuss what *unity* means and I ask, "What do you have in common with the kids who we're talking about?"

"We all need to eat," a student might respond. "We have to breathe!" So it goes, with kids usually identifying basic needs. I ask, "What are the basic needs of all humans, particularly children?" Working sometimes in small groups and sometimes as the entire class, students come up with such responses as food, shelter, clothes, water, schools, doctors, and toys. We discuss whether items are a basic need or a "desire." For example, some classes have decided that while toys may not be a basic need for children, the right to play is. Out of such a discussion come more questions, such as "What would it feel like if your basic needs were not met?" "How many kids don't have their basic needs met?" and "Is anyone doing something to help kids who don't have their basic needs met?" I encourage students to look up *children's rights* and *human rights* in our school library and on the Internet. One book that kids find is *A Children's Chorus*, published by UNICEF (1989). This beautifully illustrated book goes through the 10 principles contained in the 1959 United Nations Declaration of the Rights of the Child.

One challenge is to make sure that from the very start, such immense problems are not seen as "foreign," only occurring among "others." Thus I like to start my in-depth study of world justice issues at home. Some of my students bring to class certain stereotypes about the rest of the world, especially stereotypes they have gotten from TV and the media. Starting with problems in this country acts to counter stereotypes of "poor" Africa, Asia, and Latin America. It also centers the children in something that is familiar to many of them: poverty and homelessness in the United States.

One of my first reading/language arts units is on homelessness in the United States. I begin by displaying on my overhead projector a photo of a snowy scene in front of the White House. Before showing the caption I ask students to make observations. They ultimately are surprised that what they guessed were snow-covered rocks or garbage are actually sleeping homeless people (the photo is reproduced in Bigelow et al., 2007, p. 32). As with other photos I use, we make observations, talk about how we feel, connect it to what we already know, ask why the situation exists, and think about what might be done.

EVICTION STORIES

After this introduction, we take a few days to read Sharon Bell Mathis's (1986) *Sidewalk Story*, which tells of a family being evicted from their apartment and the role of a 9-year-old neighbor girl in fighting the eviction.

We also read Langston Hughes's "Ballad of the Landlord" and Lucille Clifton's poem "Eviction" and write some of our own poems.

I also share news stories that talk of the continuing poverty in the United States and the intense poverty in some places overseas. I find it beneficial to begin with discussion of U.S. poverty because it is close to home and virtually all my students have stories to tell about homeless people who are relatives, or whom they encounter in their neighborhoods or when they travel.

During these discussions, I occasionally find that some of my own students or members of their families are homeless. Because the stories and poetry I use portray homelessness as mainly a social problem, and not something to be ashamed of, my homeless students are usually willing to describe their situation; their classmates listen with respectful curiosity.

One year a student explained that during the summer his house burned down and he was living in a motel room with several other family members. Once he shared the story, his classmates were more sensitive to some of his moods and needs. One student assisted him in co-writing a dialogue poem between a small home, the motel room, and a big home, the apartment where his family finally relocated. In a dialogue poem, two characters talk to each other; the dialogue poem is particularly effective in getting kids to understand how things are similar yet different. (For related teaching ideas, see Bigelow et al., 2007, p. 55.)

With the children having some basic background about conditions in the United States, I feel more comfortable exploring poverty and injustice in other countries. Helping the students recognize that there is a commonality to such problems helps lay the groundwork for developing attitudes of solidarity that go beyond mere charity. In other words, I want students to recognize patterns in world problems and how those patterns are connected to problems in our own communities and country. Then students are more likely to begin to understand that working for global justice also involves changing "our" world as well, and that when we help to change conditions for "others" we are helping to change them for ourselves.

I try to help my students develop a feeling of solidarity through understanding the often-expressed notion that "no person is an island" or, as Dr. Martin Luther King Jr. put it so eloquently, "Injustice anywhere is a threat to justice everywhere." This is no simple task in a culture that glorifies individual consumption as a vehicle to personal satisfaction. My students are little different from many U.S. youth—65% of whom have TVs in their bedrooms and who watch on average nearly 25 hours of TV a week and more than 20,000 television commercials a year. I regularly challenge my students on what I label "TV addiction" and ask them to think about what they see, think, and buy.

In one activity, I place a shopping bag in front of the class and ask the students to guess what is inside. As their guesses get more accurate, I take out a T-shirt, a McDonald's Happy Meal toy, and a Nike shoe. I then ask how far these items have traveled. Initial responses are, "From McDonald's," or "From the store." As I question students, it becomes clear to them that the items were made somewhere else.

I have a student come up and read where each item is from; we then locate the country on the world map. We talk about where other things are from as we examine backpacks, shoes, and clothing. For homework, students do a "Where Are My Things From?" activity, in which they list 10 household items, the brand name, and where they are made. The next day students share lists, and then label and color maps indicating the origin of their common things.

SWEATSHOP CONDITIONS

Along with this activity I show the video *When Children Do the Work*, which graphically portrays the harsh conditions of sweatshops and how some children are robbed of their childhood. The first segment of the video is an excerpt from the National Labor Committee's *Zoned for Slavery* video, which describes sweatshop conditions in garment factories in El Salvador and Honduras. The video's narrator explains that a Gap shirt made in El Salvador sells in the United States for $20, but the workers receive just 12 cents. "Who gets the other $19.88?" the narrator demands. I later use these and other statistics for story problems in math.

The second segment of the video examines child workers in Pakistan. A carpet factory manager explains that he has 40 looms worked by 100 children and that "we chain them 3 or 4 hours a day to teach them not to run away." He adds that the children also sleep chained to their looms. My students are repelled by scenes of such oppression, but inspired by the story of Iqbal Masih, a child worker who became an activist with the Bonded Labor Liberation Front and who was killed under suspicious circumstances.

The final segment shows the Women's Network of the United Food and Commercial Workers Union leafletting a Wal-Mart store, protesting the sale of products made by 8- to 12-year-olds in Bangladesh. The workers explain why they think that such practices are both morally wrong and an attack on working people in this country. I remind my students of newspaper articles we've read about companies from our region moving to places of cheap labor, putting area workers out of work. This reinforces my emphasis on building a sense of solidarity with others around the world who are fighting economic oppression.

To further deepen children's understanding of their interconnectedness to conditions around the world, I use Bernice Reagon's song "Are My Hands Clean?" The song tells the story of a blouse that is created from the labor and resources of El Salvador, Venezuela, Trinidad, Haiti, South Carolina, and New Jersey. The children trace the route of the blouse and its raw materials on a map and contrast the wages of the workers that are described in the song.

When I first used this song I assumed that children would easily get the message of connectedness and potential responsibility that the title implies. No such luck. After playing the song I ask, "What does 'Are my hands clean?' really mean?" I receive a range of responses, including "The workers' hands get dirty in those sweatshops," "All those chemicals in the shirts must dirty our hands," "Because it's been everywhere we should wash the shirts before we wear them or our hands will get dirty," and "Maybe we're responsible for how those people have to work so hard because we buy the clothing." I tell students that the expression "to wash one's hands of something" means to take no responsibility, and I ask, "What would it mean to make our hands clean?"

I have also found that poetry is particularly useful in helping children understand comparisons and contrasts—to reinforce similarities between people and yet highlight inequalities that need to be explored. The dialogue poem is an especially good model. Sometimes, I use photos of child workers or sweatshop employees to spark the poetry writing. Working in pairs, students examine the pictures and then write a dialogue poem—between a boss and a worker, for example, or between a child worker and child student, a poor child and a rich child. Later the students share their poems with each other or with fourth-grade students during our biweekly "sharing" process. Some are included on our "Stop Child Labor and Sweatshops" bulletin board.

BROADER ECONOMIC ISSUES

I do various class activities to help students place child labor and sweatshops in the context of broader economic issues. As part of math class, I have students graph and demonstrate the disparities of wealth between continents of the world. (See Bigelow et al., 2007, p.103.) In one activity, I have each of my 25 students represent 240 million people and then spread out to assigned continents on the global map that is painted onto our school's playground. I then distribute 25 "treats" (usually cookies) according to the distribution of the world's wealth; the continents of Europe and North America get nearly two thirds of the wealth, or 17 of the 25 cookies. At times this leads to considerable dissension and cookie robbery, but also to an emotional learning experience that begins to unveil aspects of the great disparities in the distribution of wealth around the world.

Afterward, I have students write and reflect on this activity. They invariably express disbelief and outrage at, as one student put it, "how come Asia has so many people and so few cookies, I mean resources." Often the students representing North America and Europe refuse to share their treats, and this is seen as the highest form of selfishness. I then ask, "What would it mean in the real world for North America and Europe to share?"

I also want to show children that even within a country, wealth is not evenly divided. To do so, I use the "Ten Chairs of Inequality" simulation from the United for Fair Economy (see Bigelow & Peterson, 2002, p. 115). In this exercise, the U.S. population is divided into tenths and represented by 10 students. The wealth in the United States is represented by 10 chairs in the front of the classroom. We start off with each of the 10 students sitting on one chair—how the country would be if wealth were evenly distributed. I then explain that, according to U.S. government statistics, a mere 10% of the population (represented by one person) occupied 5 chairs in 1976 and 7 chairs as of 1996.

This activity elicits considerable conversation. I draw connections to earlier activities of the world distribution of resources and of sweatshops and child labor. This helps students realize that the issue isn't just disparities in wealth between different countries but disparities within countries as well, in particular, the United States. By recognizing that great divisions of wealth exist both within our country and throughout the world, students begin to see that problems can have common roots, thus further nourishing the seeds of solidarity. They can begin to see that the problem is not so much a division of wealth and power between countries as it is a division of wealth and power between social classes.

One year, students were so interested in pursuing these issues that they asked to set up what became the "No Child Labor Club," which ultimately included third, fourth and fifth graders. The club did additional research, made posters, circulated a petition, and eventually participated in a local march sponsored by labor organizations against NAFTA and sweatshops. A couple of my students spoke at the rally, which started at our school and marched to a nearby factory that had moved its operations to Mexico. Even though my students focused almost exclusively on the issue of child labor, they were among the most warmly received speakers. Keshia Hernandez, a fifth-grade student at the time, told the crowd of about

150 people that she hated child labor. "I will spread my feelings around the world," she promised.

Keshia had heard my story about my experience in Egypt. How much of it she remembered I don't know. I do know, however, that although the question of "why" that flows from that story may never be adequately answered, there are other important questions that elementary students can wrestle with and begin to answer. Questions such as, Why is the world the way it is? and What can we do to make it a more just place? Through such questioning, the seeds of solidarity will hopefully take hold and begin to flourish.

NOTE

This chapter is reprinted from *Rethinking Schools, 15*(2), Winter, 2000/2001.

REFERENCES

Bigelow, B., & Peterson, B. (2002). *Rethinking globalization: Teaching for justice in an unjust world*. Milwaukee: Rethinking Schools.

Bigelow, B., et al. (2007). *Rethinking our classrooms: Teaching for equity and justice* (Vol. 1). Milwaukee: Rethinking Schools.

Mathis, S. (1986). *Sidewalk story*. New York: Puffin.

UNICEF. (1989). *A children's chorus*. New York: Dutton.

PART III

Teaching About Race, Ethnicity, and Language

CHAPTER 7

Revisiting the Struggle for Integration

Michelle Fine and Bernadette Anand

THE PROJECT we describe in this essay emerged from thinking about Fridays. While the Monday-through-Thursday schedule at Renaissance Middle School in Montclair, New Jersey, covers the traditional distribution of curriculum, Fridays are dedicated to 9-week cycles of 2-hour sessions. Each session involves in-depth work focusing on five themes: Aviation; Genetics; Building Bridges; Community Service; and this, the Civil Rights Oral History Project. Because the school is thematically organized around core notions of justice, history, social movements, and "renaissances" (that is, Italian, Harlem, and Montclair), we structured this project around the deeply contested history of the desegregation of the Montclair public schools.

Renaissance Middle School, like all schools in Montclair, enjoys rich racial and ethnic diversity, the town having been a court-ordered site for desegregation. As of this writing, the school is just 3 years old, with 225 sixth-, seventh-, and eighth-grade students, balanced evenly by gender and by race, with African American and White the primary "racial" codes relied upon by the district. The student body is also diverse in terms of social class, with just under 20% of students eligible for free or reduced-price lunch.

In a state recognized as the fourth most racially segregated in the nation, in a town well known for its racially integrated schools, Renaissance is committed to serious intellectual work as well as racial and economic equity. Students' curricula are project based and interdisciplinary, and the school is explicitly detracked, with 8:00 a.m. to 4:00 p.m. school days. Resources and personnel are directed primarily at instruction: teachers, adults from the community, adjuncts, and parent volunteers are relentlessly dedicated to providing strong academic support so that all students can perform meaningful inquiry-based work.

The Civil Rights Oral History project was not, politically or pedagogically, a departure from the ethical or intellectual stance of the school. As progressive educators, eager for students to engage with historic and contemporary struggles for racial and economic justice, we believed the Civil Rights Oral History Project would prove to be an effective learning experience. Dr. Bernadette Anand was invited to serve as principal of Renaissance on the basis of her reputation as a progressive teacher and principal, a radical critic of tracking, and a supporter of student-based inquiry and multiculturalism; Michelle Fine, a university faculty member, was a parent/volunteer. Together, we constructed the course in that uneasy balance between educator-structured and student-directed learning. As the students moved forward, they learned about local history and about themselves as excavators of a history rarely told. In this chapter, we chronicle the course while identifying key critical turning points and unresolved issues.

We began with a quick immersion into the history of the struggle. We arranged to have *The Montclair Times* scanned for articles relevant to desegregation during the years 1947 to 1972. On the first day of each cycle, students individually reviewed the local newspaper articles tracing Montclair's history of segregation and integration, lawsuits, "riots," the school board plans for incremental integration, the denials of racism, the development of magnet schools, and tracking, as well as the stubbornly persistent racial and economic gaps in academic achievement. As they reviewed the newspapers, they began to ask questions along these lines:

Why is the Black Student Association protest called a riot—but when the White parents get together to fight integration it's just a parents' meeting?

This town is not only segregated by race, but also by wealth. Which was the problem?

Why do we still sit separately in the lunchroom?

Did the kids have a problem with integration or was it just the parents?

After some initial instruction and discussion, students were quick to point out the biases of the articles, the journalistic "slants" that accompanied the reporting of the "facts." Some students, particularly a few African American boys, noticed a disparaging tone toward African American "student protests" which was absent in the paper's descriptions of White parents' "meetings." Others noted the frequent placement of articles about the Black Student Association near articles about liquor store robberies or drug busts. A few commented that "winners usually write the history." Others concluded, "That's why we have to do this project." Even in the early stages of the project, conflicts arose as we discussed past controversies. We strove to set a distinct tone: one of respect for all points of view.

In preparation for the interviews, we watched portions of *Eyes on the Prize*, read *Freedom's Children*, and discussed these histories of racism in two Southern states, Arkansas and Alabama. Students were shocked by the brutality of Little Rock and awed by the strength shown by protesters and those who refused to take no for an answer. The class then listened to Montclair's own Arthur Kinoy, civil rights activist and lawyer, who riveted us with national and local stories about oppression, resistance, and McCarthyism. Kinoy's enthusiasm came across in the laughter that punctuated his tough talk of blacklisting, institutional and state-sponsored exclusions. He reminded us that struggle and protest are lifelong work. Students soon learned that it wasn't only the South that was ambivalent about or hostile to integration. As they read and reread the newspapers, they came to see the use of phrases such as *neighborhood schools, worries about small children on buses,* or *community control* as polite ways for community members to insist on segregated schools. Students quickly saw how fundamentally race was inscribed in the history of our town.

With the archive of these articles in hand, the class worked together to produce a time line of the major segregation and desegregation events. From the creation of this time line onward, the structure of the course evolved according to the students' interests. They identified key players from the newspaper articles and then recruited widely for a broad sample of potential interviewees. Early in the fall, a small group of students wrote a letter that appeared in the local newspaper inviting bus drivers, teachers, students, crossing guards, shopkeepers, parents, children, and teachers who observed or participated in the late 1960s integration struggles to contact the school for an interview. More than 20 interviews were completed during the course of the school year.

With our guidance and that of their peers, students prepared themselves for the interview process. They generated the questions to be asked and role-played the passive or reticent interviewee as well as the one who wouldn't shut up. We explained that oral history interviews should be designed to elicit personal stories, filled with contradiction, varied perspectives, and layered experiences. We sought variety, not consensus. We were all surprised at the level of sophistication and honesty that students brought to the project, as evidenced by the tough questions they composed: "Did the teachers take out their anger on you because you were 'colored'?" "Did other kids, I mean White kids, invite you to their house for dinner?" "Were you upset that your parents brought a lawsuit?"

In preparing for the interviews, there was a long and sometimes difficult conversation about language, focusing specifically on whether students should use *colored, Negro* (the vernacular of the times), *black,* or *African American* in the interviews. One student asked if it would be appropriate to use *Nigger,* a term he relies upon to signal endearment and friendship, seemingly naive about its history. The class argued with varied points of view. We decided, ultimately, out of respect for our interviewees, we wouldn't use *Nigger,* but *colored* or *Negro* would be acceptable if the interviewees used that language first.

Later in the year, this conversation was resurrected, this time specifically about the use of *Nigger* or *Nigga,* by and among African American boys and their music. Allie Baskerville, the grandson of one of the women who initially brought the lawsuit for desegregation in 1967, had just conducted a phone interview with his grandmother about the litigation. After hanging up, he turned to Bernadette and some friends and asked, almost innocently, "You know, given what my grandmother and her friends did, how come we use *Nigger* so easily, when it was used to put us down?"

Students were also surprised and provoked by some of the interview material. They expected stories about discrimination from Whites and solidarity among Blacks. But when the students asked a number of the then–Negro children, "Were the White children nice to you?" they were surprised to hear from two respondents, "Some of the White children were better friends to me than some of the other Negro children." A difficult conversation ensued as White, African American, and biracial children wondered, "Why would other Black children be mad that you were doing well in school, and resent that you were a cheerleader?" Two African American students admitted that it was "hard to talk about that in front of some of the White kids." Stories of intraracial struggles moved to the surface, sharing the floor with stories of interracial conflicts. On a visit to Renaissance, an African American teacher from Connecticut admitted to her discomfort when she listened to a light-skinned respondent recall, "I remember being invited, often, to many White homes for sleepovers . . ." This teacher recalled White girls' shunning her in the 1950s. "Try havin' nappy hair and real dark skin and see if you got invited," she remarked to the class. Her comments sparked conversations about skin color, "good hair," and who gets invited to which sleepovers.

And then there were just the chilling, recognizable historic revelations about our town that shivered through the class. During an interview with Lydia Davis-Barrett, once a child in the Montclair public schools and currently the director of the Essex County Urban League, students learned:

"So we decided to go to the white people's pool to take lessons—boy, were they surprised to see us, but they just said, 'You sure you're in the right place?' to which we said that we were sure. But what hurt me so, as I approached the pool, is that I realized in the colored people's pool we had to dip our feet in a bucket of disinfectant. . . . no such rule in the White people's pool."

Davis-Barrett continued: "I graduated first in my class, or so I thought, from Glenfield and then I got to the high school and I was getting Ds. I didn't understand it, and my father was mad. He tried to find out what was going on. Was I messing up? Were the teachers racist? And then he discovered that I was first in my class, at least first among the colored children, but we were given a 'colored' curriculum at Glenfield. We weren't getting the same rigor, the same courses as the White children, so of course once I got to the high school I was way behind. . . . My dad wanted to bring a lawsuit but he was a civil servant and they told him if he did, he would lose his job." Students sat stunned and openmouthed. Some were disbelieving, while others were familiarly pained.

An important set of pedagogical turns emerged as we recognized the unconscious assumptions that infused our work. When students sympathetically asked some of the children of activists, "Was it difficult being the child of an activist?" they learned that their worries were misguided. We had all assumed that the litigation was difficult and embarrassing, and we prepared questions that were appropriately sensitive. However, most of the men and women who were intimately involved said the lawsuit was "thrilling. . . . I knew they [my parents] loved me because they were willing to take up the fight." We had to go back to our interview protocol and reassess the biases in all of our questions and search for other buried assumptions.

In interviews with African American and White men and women educators, parents, activists, then children in the schools, we heard detailed stories of White resistance to integration, some surprising White support for integration and opposition to community schools, complex reactions to desegregation within the African American community, and the delights and the vulnerabilities of having a "mixed" group of friends. We heard about "colored" support for integration and about economic and political tensions within the Black community. We learned about housing segregation seemingly so hard to undo that schools became the site of the struggle for desegregation. We questioned why the schools built in the "Negro" section of town were so well equipped with gyms, equipment, theaters, and music and dance studios, especially compared with the schools in the "White" section of town. We then realized that the school board assumed, and they were probably right, that some White people had to be bribed into putting their children on a bus to go to the "other" side of town. Throughout the interviews, it seemed painfully clear that most White children were going to get a good education, integration or not. On the other hand, African American students who had lost opportunities during segregation experienced a new kind of racism, confronted a more veiled form of segregation through tracking, even after the victory in 1967.

A memorable moment came when students interviewed Dr. Mindy Fullilove. A psychiatrist at Columbia Presbyterian, Dr. Fullilove is the daughter of a civil rights activist from a neighboring town, the daughter who used to "skip to school as a young child, loving every day." She knew as a child that her father was involved with a civil rights struggle in his town of Orange, New Jersey. She didn't know, however, that if he won, she would have to go to school with White children. He won. Dr. Fullilove told the seventh graders, "Integration almost killed me." At that moment we realized that an unspoken, unchallenged bias floated in the room and saturated our interviews: that segregation was bad and integration was good. Unacknowledged was the pain, the loss, the questionable consequences of integration, especially for African American children, families, and teachers. We spent much time reviewing how every so-called solution to social injustice brings with it other burdens, other struggles. We realized that African Americans in the Americas can never rest assured that racism has been put in its place. Just as painful, we saw that racism and White supremacy do not disappear after integration; they merely take new forms.

But insights never come easily and they don't come to everyone at the same time in the same way. There were significant points of dissensus among us for which we, as educators, had to create room and respect, as well as analysis. For example, Kaelin (White girl) and Trevor (biracial boy) argued powerfully and with conviction about how to ask about "teachers" after integration. Kaelin preferred what she thought was a "neutral" question such as, "What were the teachers like after integration?" Trevor preferred what he thought was a more directed, even sharply pointed question: "Did the teachers take out their anger on you because you were colored?" We spent a full session discussing the politics of their questions and why Kaelin would want "nice" data and Trevor might want evidence of struggle. Kaelin knew she was looking for some evidence of White adults who fought against racism and Trevor knew he was looking for evidence about the pain of integration. Both knew that if they didn't ask (for the good news or the bad), these memories might never be reported. We asked the question both ways and got wildly different responses. We recognized that how you ask a question affects what you get in response.

A few weeks later, students in the class were asked to describe the project to a newspaper reporter from *The Newark Star-Ledger* who had learned about the project through the students' open letter to *The Montclair Times*. Here, too, the students' racialized postures were evident. One White student said, "It was interesting, really, to hear that people in town didn't know the schools were segregated. They didn't know anything was wrong." An African American boy interrupted, "Lots of people knew something was wrong but they didn't know what to do about it." Even at the end of the year, in thinking about the dramatic differences between interviews with White and African American women activists, we continued to note the differences in our own reactions to what we were hearing. Michelle asked, "What differences did you notice in these interviews?" A White girl responded, "It was harder for White people to be involved in the protests because they lost friends." At the same moment an African American boy responded, "White people who were involved took all the credit." We analyzed again what the women said in the interviews and then what we heard. In our analysis we noticed a story within a story: a tale of race, class, and gender in our past and a tale of race, class, and gender in our midst. That is, we spent much time trying to figure out how each of the interviewees and each of us constructs narratives of our lives and our politics; how profoundly our race, class, and gender positions influence what we hear, and how we frame and interpret issues of social (in)justice.

Throughout the year, students came to see that what is taken for granted today in their lives has a long history of national and local struggles. Some went home and asked their parents about going to Montclair High School in the 1960s. Others gathered stories about segregated schools in the South. They started to question their own lunchroom and their future. What's going to happen when we hit high school—will we "split" again by race? Why were some Whites so scared to go to school with Blacks? Why were some Black students so hard on other Black children who were academic achievers? Why were there so few Black educators then and still today? As educators, Bernadette and Michelle noticed that there were, and are, conversations still too terrifying to wander into, assumptions too horrifying to challenge, such as, What counts as smart—and is it genetic? What about all those teachers who encouraged some students to believe they were smart and others to believe they were not adequate? What are the peer costs of being academically engaged for African American children? How do we make sense of the racial segregation of special education? What does it mean to be biracial, part White and part Black, or part Asian and part Black, or part White and part Latino, in this conversation? Why is "basic skills" so segregated? How does social class interact with race and ethnicity in this town, and in this country? Why do people judge students whose friends are from different races? What happens when we have to decide whose music to play at the dance? And ultimately, we all had to reflect on a question we didn't entertain at the beginning of the year: Is integration really better?

For some students, this project simply reiterated a history of struggle that has been their family's history of struggle. It was in their blood, their legacy, discussed over the dinner table. For others it was new and painful, awkward, or even embarrassing. White students and educators had to figure out what kind of legacy we brought to the table; African American students and educators had to confront tough evidence of separation, hatred, and denial of opportunity burned into their collective memory; biracial students, and Asian and Latino students, had to carve a place for themselves in this history. All students had to assess their own relation to this struggle. No one, of course, wanted to see themselves or their kin as "bad guys," eager to perpetuate unequal racial and economic opportunities. But then the conversation turned to what you do if you witness unequal or unfair treatment of a student by a teacher, by another classmate, or a by stranger. Do you simply watch and turn? Do you intervene? Do you tell a teacher? Do you encourage it?

"By witnessing passively," someone remarked, "if we do nothing, then it keeps going on. I mean, we allow it to get worse." And so these young people in the 1990s, the children of the generation who fought so many of these battles, by year's end began to confront the ongoing politics of race, class, and gender. To this list they added the politics of "being fat," "having bad clothes," "stuttering," "not being very masculine," "they say I'm gay," "not having a mother," "having big breasts," and, as always, "where we sit in the lunchroom."

Months into the course, three African American boys from sixth and seventh grade were stopped by the police while walking home. Their backpacks were searched. Apparently a passerby had called the police and said that a group of boys—one of whom had a gun—were throwing snowballs. Unsuspecting, these boys had stopped to purchase some gum. When the police insisted that they stand still to be frisked, a young White girl from Renaissance, on her way to dance class, saw the confrontation. She had her mother call Bernadette Anand immediately because she knew something was wrong. She would not "witness passively."

As it turned out, the boys were entirely innocent and the police were asked to come to the school to speak with the school community, including the three boys and their parents. Students, parents, and faculty across the school engaged in an analysis of the history, politics, and practices of police harassment of children of color. This occurred only 2 days after the Amadou Diallo murder in New York City, when an innocent African man was gunned down by police, killed with more than 40 bullets, in a case of mistaken identification.

Today, students and faculty are organizing a strategy for a delegation of Renaissance students and faculty to visit stores that are "discriminately suspect" of youths. Some students are conducting community-based research in which White and African American students enter a particular store and the "researcher" documents who is followed, who is asked to leave, who is offered help. They are keeping notes, honing their research and activist skills.

We are now well beyond the years of formal segregation, post–civil rights, thriving in a town well known for its embrace of integration. Indeed, Montclair has been recognized by *New Jersey Magazine* as one of the "nation's best towns for multi-racial families." Yet boys of color are still particularly vulnerable to police surveillance and harassment. But what separates this school from most is that here the administration and faculty decided that this police search constituted an assault against the school-wide community, an issue in need of historical and social analysis, a dynamic to be studied and halted. A White girl witnessed and reported. The three boys and their families were embraced by a school collectively experiencing the pain. An African American police officer came to address the school, relating his own experiences of brutality suffered as a youth at the hands of police officers, noting that that was the moment when he decided to become an officer himself. At Renaissance Middle School, as part of their formal and informal educations, young people across racial and ethnic groups, across economic categories and neighborhoods, learn intimately and critically about the scars of exclusion and oppression, in the past as well as today. They learn, too, that research, resistance, and community organizing are an ongoing part of life for those concerned with social justice.

When we think now about the class, we notice an interesting pattern. In the fall, there was, discernibly, uneven participation. African American boys were much more likely to be involved in the classroom conversations than any other demographic "group" in the room: eager to talk, interview, generate questions, and probe more fully. While everyone participated some—given the nature of the project, everyone had to generate questions and conduct interviews—initially it seemed toughest for some of the White boys to engage. Understanding discrimination firsthand or even secondhand from family and friends were critical "assets" in this project. Students who had an "eye" for injustice, had been educated around the dinner table or perhaps had been scrutinized by mall security and surveillance, were most ready to do the research and analysis. Over time, however, with practice at interviewing and being interviewed, independent researching, and analyzing of the transcripts, engagement was much more even. Eventually, whether they were creating questions, conducting interviews, transcribing, writing the preface for their collection of interviews (*Montclair Wrong for Too Long: The Struggles for Integration*), or figuring out the table of contents, most students became actively engaged, demonstrating their curiosity and wisdom.

On the last morning of the interviewing phase of the project, two women were scheduled for interviews. We spoke first with a White woman, now retired, who fought hard for integration as a mother of an adolescent in the early 1970s. We then talked to an older African American woman, a university professor, who also fought hard, at the same time, as a parent and community member. Each was asked, in seventh-grade dialect, "So, was life better before integration or after?" The first woman, without hesitation, exclaimed, "Much better after! The students go to school together, they have play dates, they are no longer separated." And the second woman explained, after a long pause, "Neither was better. The struggle continues." Students learned that both answers were, in their time and for each of these women, respectively, "true."

COURSE MATERIALS

The Montclair Times, indexed from 1947 through 1972 for all articles related to desegregation.

Haskins, J. (1998). *Separate but not equal: The dream and the struggle*. New York: Scholastic.

Levine, E. (1993). *Freedom's children: Young civil rights activists tell their own stories*. New York: Avon.

No easy walk. (1986). *Eyes on the prize* [PBS Video]. Virginia.

CHAPTER 8

A High School Class on Race and Racism

Lawrence Blum

FOR MOST people, "Cambridge, Massachusetts" conjures up images of world-class universities and, more recently, through-the-roof housing prices. But Cambridge Rindge and Latin (CRLS), the city's only public high school, located a mere three blocks from Harvard Yard, represents an entirely different segment of Cambridge life. The school, of approximately 1,850 students in 2003, is home to a remarkable economic, racial, ethnic, and linguistic diversity—42.3% Black, 33.7% White (including students of Arab or other Middle Eastern background), 15.1% Latino, and 8.4% Asian American; 40% low income; approximately 60 different home languages. The Cambridge area also hosts an impressive array of private (and parochial) schools, and very few Cambridge-resident Harvard and MIT professors send their children to CRLS.

I have taught a course on race and racism at the high school three times, most recently in the fall of 2002. Normally, I teach race studies, multiculturalism, and moral philosophy at UMass/Boston. I have no training as a high school teacher, but because my children attend(ed) the high school, and through a quirky set of circumstances, I ended up with my own class there in spring 1999. I was curious whether high school students would be willing to discuss racial issues in an open and honest way across racial and ethnic boundaries—an endeavor that, in my experience, most college students, and adults as well, find quite difficult. I hoped to be able to create a comfortable and trusting atmosphere that, leavened with a bit of humor, would facilitate this goal. And, indeed, I found high school students extremely, even dauntingly, open with their views and feelings about race and racism, and anything else for that matter. I do not want to generalize beyond my limited experience, but I have found that my students are grateful for an opportunity to discuss, explore, and learn about race-related matters; that they are very interested in each other's opinions, especially though not only across racial and ethnic lines; and that Black and Latino students will express themselves more freely in a class in which they are the majority than they report doing in other enriched and advanced classes in which they are less than about 20%.

I will discuss the course and the class in more detail but first want to situate my experience within wider currents of educational reform that have been playing out in Cambridge and the nation. The racial "achievement gap" has come onto the national screen in the past few years. Whites and Asians outperform Blacks and Latinos in school to a significant and troubling extent. The literature on this phenomenon is vast. Popular theories among conservatives and traditional liberals are that Black kids castigate high achievers as "acting White" (Fordham & Ogbu, 1986; Ogbu, 2002). Race liberals and radicals tend to favor Claude Steele's (Steele & Aronson, 1998) "stereotype threat" hypothesis, according to which Black students capable of high achievement fail because their fear of confirming what they rightly recognize to be a culturally salient stereotype of Blacks as low achievers leads them to become rattled in test situations, and so to underperform.[1]

The achievement gap shows up between different kinds of schools—roughly, suburban White and urban Black and Latino schools—and within mixed schools as well. In discussions in my UMass education classes, I find that students who have not studied the issue think the gap is primarily a matter of class—urban students don't do as well because their economic circumstances hinder them in various ways. But class cannot be the only factor, since the racial gap exists within the same income groups too, and is in fact greater among upper-middle-class than working-class Whites and Blacks, though it is not as great as when both middle-class Whites and Asians are compared with working-class and poor Blacks and Latinos.

In recent years, the racial achievement gap has become much discussed at CRLS. The school is part of the national Minority Student Achievement Network, which consists of schools with a demographic similar to that of CRLS that are attempting to close the achievement gap. CRLS has a sizable White working-class population, generally of Portuguese origin (often fairly recent immigrants), as well as Irish and Italian, along with a larger White middle-class group. There are middle-class Black and Latino students as well, although they are a small percentage of those respective groups. As far as I know, achievement measures are not generally broken down by class, and discussion in settings in which I have been present often conflate class with race.

The advanced placement (AP) classes are a major, particularly visible locus of the achievement issue at the high school. Nationally, in recent years, these classes have become increasingly important as indicators of both school reputation and student college admissions cachet. Hence they are seen as the site of "excellent education." These classes tend, at CRLS, to be about 80–90% White and Asian, although in recent years there has been a concerted effort, partly successful, to bring more Black and Latino students into some AP subjects and to offer more sections of them. At the outset of the course, 7 of my students (of 16 present) cited the lack of "minority" kids in AP classes as "the major racial issue in the school." (*Minority* is the term of choice, both officially and by self-attribution, for all non-White students. More on this below.)

The achievement gap has also become an integral part of White parent community discourse in Cambridge in the past 5 years or so, though sometimes in indirect ways. A popular theme among those who see the gap as morally and politically unacceptable is the "two communities" narrative. This narrative assumes that prior to the reform efforts that began at the school in the late 1990s in order to create more heterogeneously grouped classes, the school was doing a very good job of serving one "community," middle-class Whites, but a poor job of serving another "community," working-class Blacks and Latinos. (The absence, noted above, of working-class Whites in this conversation—as well as at the parent meetings where these issues have been discussed—is striking.)

The two-communities narrative is, nevertheless, preferable to the way achievement issues are more frequently framed in parent meetings at the school. For as long as I can remember, those meetings have been completely dominated by professional, educated Whites, who generally constitute 90% of those in attendance (though the advent of a new African American principal in 2002, and of a veteran CRLS African American vice principal, seems to promise a new empowerment of African American parents). In these meetings, children committed to learning (who are virtually always the children of the parents in attendance) are contrasted with those who are not; the former are "held back" and "bored" because of the latter. This is the main complaint about the heterogeneous classes, and it is a constant refrain among White, educated parents. This discourse is almost never explicitly racialized, but for the most part, the serious, hardworking kids are taken to be White and the others Black and Latino; everyone knows this reference, but no one explicitly mentions it. By contrast, the aforementioned two-communities discourse tends to explicitly bring out the racial dimension of the "well served" and the "poorly served."

The issue of heterogeneous grouping is indeed a complex one. While some research supports the general notion that heterogeneity benefits the lower-effort group without harming the higher-effort group, many committed teachers at the school clearly feel that they themselves are able to do a better job in more homogeneous classrooms (at whatever level), and the experience of the class's moving too slowly is an all too real one for many high-achieving students (Oakes, 1985; Wheelock, 1992). I feel somewhat conflicted about the issue in general, and the achievement gap it is meant to address is a very serious educational concern for which social, political, and economic reform is clearly essential, along with multifaceted educational, communal, and familial initiatives. I can only say that in my own class, students of different racial and ethnic backgrounds, and spanning a range of high and low effort and previous achievement, learned a good deal from each other in a way what neither the "two communities" nor the "my kid is bored" narrative expresses. My class contained students who went on to Yale, and others who went to community college, or to no college at all (at least in the year after high school). In a range of subjects such as literature, social studies, and arts, in which different backgrounds tend to ground different experiences, sensibilities, perspectives, and opinions, the Yale-bound students had a good deal to learn from the community college bound (and vice versa); parents of the former who prefer, or do not mind, their children's attending the bulk of their classes with students of a similar background are missing an important dimension of formal and informal education that their students could have in more mixed classes.

Let me illustrate with just one fairly typical class discussion. We had read an article (Lewin, 2002) about three girls of different races who were friends in junior high but started drifting apart in high school. This led to a discussion about social separation by race and also about kids acting in ways associated with racial groups other than their own, especially White kids "acting Black" and Black kids "acting White." (Later, we questioned this way of talking.) Here is some of the conversation, reconstructed from notes taken by a postdoctoral student who was observing the class:

> Lauren (White): It isn't that White kids really like different kinds of parties than Black kids; but they are expected to like that kind of party, so they are told who they should hang out with.
>
> Grace (Black): If someone [Black] comes down on you for "acting White," you can just ignore that if you are comfortable with yourself.
>
> Angela (Black): I went to Boston public schools until the fifth grade. When I came to Cambridge was the first time I was told I was "acting White." I knew what I was [i.e., Black]; I had been that way for 11 years. [Class laughs.]
>
> DeAnna (Black): It is easier for a White kid to hang out with Blacks if he doesn't act Black; same for Blacks with Whites. . . .

Black kids who act White aren't as accepted by other Black
kids; like if they speak proper English.[2]

WAHEED (Middle Eastern): Sometimes people just unconsciously
talk the way the people around them are talking, not because
they are consciously trying to get in with that group. My father
is Iraqi and when he is with other Iraqis he goes into this
heavy Arabic accent; I can't even understand him. It isn't a
conscious thing.

ANGELA (Black): The first time I saw Lauren in 10th grade, she
looked White but she acted Black. [Lauren blushes.]

JEANIE (Black) [affably says that Angela shouldn't run Lauren
down (although Angela was actually praising Lauren).]

EFRIEM (Black): A lot of time, a person who is acting a certain way
is only trying to make sure the other group understands him;
he isn't trying to be a certain way [i.e., not trying to get in
with that group].

GRACE (Black): I think Blacks sometimes feel that Whites are
taking their culture away, when they act Black.

(I suggest that White kids "acting Black" is a sign of the power and
influence of Black culture.)

LASHAWNA (Black): I see Whites acting Black not as influencing but
mocking. Like when we read about Native American team
names ["Braves," "Chiefs"] at the beginning of the course.
Native Americans were insulted, but the people who made up
the names thought they were fine or even flattering.

JEANIE (Black): Like Justin Timberlake of N'Sync putting Black
females in his videos. That isn't Black culture influencing
anything; it's Whites ripping off Black culture to make money.

CARL (White): [Mutters (but I make him say it out loud) that
White people have to steal other people's culture, because they
don't have any of their own.]

It is fascinating to see the Black students struggling with these issues
and coming up with such divergent views. They are trying to analyze their
own practices of inclusion and exclusion, with value judgments about those
practices hovering close by. The White students are as well. All are speaking from a distinct, race-related experience, though their resultant opinions are quite diverse. This sort of discussion is very unlikely to take place
in the kind of classes the White, educated parents envision, and both the
White and the Black and Latino students, indeed all students, thereby miss
an intellectually enriching experience.[3]

I see my course as engaging with the achievement gap issue in that I do not want the course to be yet another advanced-level class for White and Asian students. The school allows me to do some picking and choosing among the students who sign up above the 20 student limit, and I try, as I say in the course description, for a class that mirrors the racial demography of the school. (In 2002, I had nine Black students, six Whites, three Latino/Hispanics, one "Middle Eastern" [Iraqi/Iranian], and one Indian Muslim.[4]) Not all the students who end up in the class are totally committed to the subject matter. Some are simply looking for a one-semester elective or to find something that fits their schedule. A few are attracted to the "UMass" designation in the full catalogue title of the course. Some are steered by a guidance counselor or teacher who thinks the experience would be good for them.

I have at least four goals for the class. The first and main one is to offer an academically enriched course for minority students in a setting in which they are the majority of the class. The main reading for the course is college-level work on race (drawn from my college class of the same title), requiring a level of conceptual sophistication that some students have to struggle to take on. (See the "Course Materials" section below.) Very occasionally, I have had a student who was really unable to do the work and dropped the class, although I have never actually encouraged a student to drop, but have always tried to provide extra tutoring to make up for previous educational deficits. Of course, not every student identifies with the "minority" label in a way that provides an identification across non-White racial and ethnic groups; perhaps some Latino students, for example, feel as uncomfortable in my class as they do in a class of almost all White students. But the discourse of "minority" is so strong in the school that I doubt most of them experience it this way. From conversations with students and teachers at the school, I had the impression that the Black students, who are generally 40–45% of the class, are infrequently in a class this demanding in which they constitute anything like that percentage.[5] I see this course as my small contribution to closing the achievement gap.

Second, I want White students to have an experience of an academically challenging class in which they are a minority, partly so that they will empathize with the comparable situation of students of color in their AP classes (although some of the White students are not in AP classes), and partly so that they will have an experience of seeing the diversity of opinion within the minority, especially Black, group. Third, I want all the students to come to recognize that racial issues are a matter of serious academic study, not only of something personally or emotionally important. Finally, I want to help validate the experiences of discrimination, stereotyping, and stigmatization that the students of color may have experienced in the wider society and possibly in the school.

Much of the course work is historical—what in contemporary academic parlance would be called the "historical construction of race." We look at slavery and the slave trade, the displacement and killing of Native peoples, and the progressive formation of the idea of "race" from the 16th until the 19th century. We look at slavery in the Caribbean and in Spanish/Portuguese America, as well as in North America, partly to broaden the view of slavery on the part of the students, whose paradigm, unsurprisingly, is the Southern U.S. plantation system, and partly to study the contrasting systems of racial and phenotypic classification that grew up under different forms of slavery and European domination in Latin America, the Caribbean, and the United States. I try to dislodge the sense of naturalness and inevitability accompanying my (non–Latin American) students' use of racial categories in application to themselves and to society more generally.

This fairly sophisticated educational goal plays differently with different students. For example, in the middle of a unit emphasizing how Latin Americans do not think of race in terms of a "Black/White" binary and are less focused on racial classifications than U.S. Americans, Parris, a Black student, turned to Juan, an Hispanic student, and said, "Yeah, that's what I want to know. Are you guys Black, or White, or what?" By contrast, Efriem, a student of Ethiopian parents, told me in a follow-up interview I did with him after the course was over, in answer to the question "Can you say more about what you got out of the class?": "The fact that race was created, to learn that it is not inevitable or that it might not have been . . . When I participate in class where I hear people saying race is inevitable, I say no, and I am more confident about it." And Lauren, a White student involved in antiracist political activity, said that a main thing she learned in the course was that "to get rid of racism, we have to get rid of the idea of race. Before, I had believed in race but just thought we had to get rid of racism."

The historical material continually spills over into the present, and that is fine with me. Also, throughout the historical part of the course, the students do personal journals on any topic related to race. One Black boy described his and a White friend's attempt to get a job at a local art cinema and wanted to know if I thought he had been discriminated against when the friend was offered a job and he wasn't. A White (but not particularly "White looking") working-class Portuguese American girl talked about interracial relationships, decrying the narrow-mindedness of some of her friends and her family on this matter. A very racially conscious Black girl went into painful detail about the steps involved in Black females' straightening their hair. Her entry had the spirit both of informing me about something she thought I as a White male should know and probably didn't, and also expressed a combination of sympathy for and outrage toward females who undergo this process.

In addition, twice I asked the students to write about a "racial incident" they had witnessed or had been a party to. We then talked about these incidents in class (with the identities of the students hidden). A particularly interesting one was supplied by Efriem, the Black student with Ethiopian parents. He was visiting in a town in New Hampshire and entered a convenience store carrying a drink (of a type not sold in that store), looking for an item he couldn't find. The store manager followed him closely and questioned him about his drink; Efriem was sure he was being racially profiled. The class took up the question of whether the profiling had age and attire dimensions, and some White students said that White high school students, especially if they dressed in a manner associated with Black students, are also given tighter security scrutiny. Some students saw that this was itself a form of race-related profiling, although some of the non-Black students (not only White, in this case) had seen it as a nonracial form of profiling. Also, Efriem suggested that the incident was in part his own fault, for bringing the drink into the store in the first place. No other Black student would go down that particular path with him. Also, the students generally had no clear take on how to respond, how to take some kind of constructive antiracist action, in this kind of situation, for example, by challenging the manager or raising the issue with him without implying that he was necessarily guilty of any wrongdoing.

Later in the semester, we discussed contemporary racial issues—general issues in society, and issues as they arose in the school. Also, I broke the students up into racially diverse "project groups," and each group researched a topic and made a presentation at the end of the course. The topics in 2002 were comparative slave systems, academic segregation by race at the high school (i.e., the achievement gap in the context of AP classes), social segregation by race at the high school, racial profiling at the school and in the Cambridge community, and mixed-race identity.

We spent two classes on the achievement gap itself, in addition to the group presentation. For the class discussion we had read an article (Walker, 2002) about a high school in Denver—with a similar racial makeup to that of CRLS—at which, the article claimed, the guidance counselors had steered minority students away from AP classes independent of the particular student's potential. In our class discussion, students had a range of perspectives on this issue. Waheed said that at CRLS students are not discouraged from taking advanced courses. Parris said the racial tracking was the same at CRLS, only they are not open about it. (In a comparable discussion in a previous year's class, the students were much more critical of the guidance counselors for steering minority students away from the AP classes.) Jeanie, a Black student, said that students get used to lower expectations being held of them, so they are not comfortable with the high demands of the AP classes. In a later class, Jeanie went into more detail about her personal experience of this. She said she had essentially been forced, by one of her history teachers and her guidance counselor, to take an AP history class; they would not sign off on her schedule unless she agreed to sign up for that course. She said she had never taken a class that was so hard, and she just wasn't accustomed to working that hard for a course. (The particular AP course Jeanie is talking about here, however, is a famously demanding one at the high school and should not be thought of as typical of AP courses in general.) Jeanie said she was not sure that she was glad she did take the class, since she thought she would have gotten a higher grade in a non-AP class. Angela dissented from this view and said that the AP classes were manageable, that you had to push yourself a bit harder than in the other classes, but that it could be done.

Some version of Jeanie's remarks was echoed by two other Black students in my follow-up interviews. Parris, a Haitian American, said: "There are not enough Black kids who work hard. I'm not saying I'm smart, but I work hard. There are not enough Black kids who work hard. For some reason, we don't work hard enough. That's why my mother thinks African Americans are lazy." Efriem, the African immigrant Black student, said: "I would say it goes back to elementary school. The Black kids are not pushed to do that well; they don't get pushed by their parents in the same way as a lot of White kids are. By the time you get to high school you haven't had that kind of encouragement and so it is hard to do when you are a junior, to all of a sudden challenge yourself like that."

The view that minority kids did not work as hard as White kids was expressed in some form by several of the students. One White student wrote in a journal, "I don't mean to sound racist, but from what I've seen there is a large majority of minorities that don't care how they do in school." None expressed the idea that Black kids are discouraged from achieving by being said to "act White" if they are successful. However, two students mentioned a revealing twist on this idea. One Black student wrote in a journal: "I've noticed that people have formed stereotypes about people who are in AP classes. They think that they are all just smart snobby White kids, and some Black students in AP classes don't like to say that they are in the class because they don't want to be considered as 'AP' kids. It's almost as if they are embarrassed." A White student reported that students of color in AP classes do not identify themselves as "AP kids" and do not identify with the White students in those classes. Neither student suggested that students of color actually felt discouraged from signing up for these courses by the image they had of the canonical student in them, but it seems a plausible inference.

Clearly we are hearing here some age-old stereotypes of Blacks as lazy, as well as familiar and unfortunate distancing of immigrant Blacks from African Americans.[6] Later discussions and a final project about stereotypes gave the students and me an opportunity to challenge some of those stereotypes, as well as stereotyping in general. Certainly teachers' expectations also play a significant role in minority achievement, and I hoped in my own class to create a culture of demand and achievement that applied to all students alike. At the same time, unequal academic effort among different racial groups is not a mere figment of a stereotypical imagination; clearly it exists and is one contributing factor to the achievement gap. The current school administration is attempting to break the sense that this unequal effort and achievement are inevitable. Although I sometimes worry that a constant harping on the gap will subtly reinforce the idea that it is inevitable, it seems clear that recognizing the gap is a first step toward dealing with it constructively. The administration and some community groups promote events and groups targeted at Black and Latino youth that aim to encourage achievement; Parris described one such event to me in his interview, and it sounded very constructive. I also heard, more recently, that a Latino student, involved in orientation for incoming ninth graders, challenged Latino and Black students to make sure that the AP classes offered when they became juniors do not have as few of their groups as his own current AP classes did.

In my postcourse interviews with seven students, three of the five students of color talked about their own experiences in AP classes that shed light both on their experience in my class, and possibly on issues related to the achievement gap. They all said that they were aware of the very small number of minority kids—from 3 to 5 in a class of approximately 25—in those classes, and this inhibited them from speaking in the class. (At CRLS, most of these students' other classes would have had a minority of White students.) Efriem said: "I always felt like every time I spoke, people were seeing me as an example of other Blacks. I always felt like I had to represent our people." (He added, later, "You have to prove you are worthy to be there.")

Ahmad, from an Indian immigrant family, had a similar reaction. "Like, in my AP history class now [the semester following my class], there are only 4 minority and the other 26 are white. We don't really want to talk; I am not really sure why but we just don't talk. . . . Like I would think twice before answering because if I said something stupid then people would be saying, what is he doing here, why is he in the AP class." Parris, discussing an AP literature class, said, "Like, you gotta watch out. Make sure if you say something bad. You don't want to give them a negative impact of Black people. They act like we're like the first Black people they've ever met."

Several students discussed one particular such course, with a White teacher who was very eager for the students of color to participate in class but, according to my students, found this difficult to achieve. We had discussed this course in my class, and a Latino student, Vanessa, who was accustomed to being in White-dominated classes, was shocked to discover that her classmates from my class who had taken the class in question had felt uncomfortable speaking up in this class, given the teacher's encouragement. Clearly there are complex issues of identity and critical mass involved in the levels of comfort students feel in different classes. For example, this Latino girl thinks of herself very distinctly as "a minority" (again, the term of choice at the high school) and assumed that because she herself felt comfortable speaking up, other "minority" kids would do so as well. Ahmad, who did not feel comfortable, also, like Vanessa, distinctly saw himself as a "minority" (although the South Asians, and other Asian students as well, often do not identify with the Black and Latino students). Perhaps Ahmad's particular way of appropriating a "minority" identity was bound up with his growing up in a largely Black and Latino housing project in Cambridge. He had adopted some hip-hop cultural mannerisms and felt comfortable with the Blacks and Latinos. While Vanessa infers from her comfort in speaking that other minority students will feel such comfort as well, Ahmad (in no way a shy student) feels inhibited by what he perceives as a lack of a critical mass of minority students.

At the same time, both Efriem and Parris articulate a distinct sense of racial vulnerability absent in both Ahmad and Vanessa. Both say they are worried that a "stupid" remark they make will make Blacks look bad in general; Ahmad says only that he is worried that a stupid remark he makes will make students wonder why he is there, not members of a specific racial or ethnic group. The Black students' responses are akin to Steele's idea of stereotype threat, except that the students do not say that they performed less well on the graded assignments in the class, but only that they did not feel as comfortable speaking.

At the end of my course quite a few students suggested that the course should be mandatory (though some also recognized that this would make for a very different atmosphere in the class). One Black student said, "Things you would want to say in other classes you can say in this class." And another: "Other teachers are not as educated about it. It isn't that they don't want to talk about it." This suggests to me that many high school students, not only the few in my own class, are eager to engage with racial issues in a thoughtful and nondogmatic manner, if a safe and respectful

context can be provided for doing so, one in which there is a critical mass
of the relevant groups. Some students thought that several of their teachers would actually like to have more conversations about racial topics but
were either not sufficiently knowledgeable to do so, or not sure they could
handle the emotions that might emerge in such discussions. The high
school is currently engaging these issues in some helpful ways. As mentioned, racial issues are increasingly part of the school's discourse about
education, and the school has always offered several courses on African
American history and other race-related topics. In 2003–2004, Peggy
McIntosh's project Seeking Educational Equality and Diversity (SEED) ran
groups for parents, teachers, and administrators, and this initiative will be
carried into the future. I believe that many teachers at the school are eager
to take on the challenges suggested by my students' comments above.

On the more challenging issue of the "achievement gap," I cannot
draw conclusions from my minor foray into the high school world. I can
only hope and assume that caring and knowledgeable teachers who try
their best to genuinely reject the racist assumptions about the intellectual
capacities of Black and Latino students to which we are all subject, and
who can hold all their students to high standards of achievement while
providing the support essential to meeting those standards, can help move
us in the right direction.[7]

NOTES

1. See, for example, Steele and Aronson (1998), pp. 401–427. Jencks and
Phillips's (1998) collection presents and evaluates many hypotheses about the
achievement gap (focused more specifically on the gap in standardized test scores).
Genetically based explanations, suggested by the 1994 best-seller *The Bell Curve*,
by Richard Herrnstein and Charles Murray, are refuted by Jencks and Phillips in
the introduction to their collection and do not seem to be taken seriously by the
scholarly community dealing with the achievement gap.

2. The students frequently referred to what I would call "standard English"
as "proper English," and "African American vernacular" as "slang." I did not systematically challenge this use but intend to do so next time I teach the class, in
fall 2004.

3. This discussion, like so many in the course of the term, was intense and
very fast moving, and I was unable in the moment to take up various threads
that might have seemed to cry out for more exploration, such as the idea that
Whites have no culture, or reasons other than those mentioned why a member
of one group might adopt or be attracted to the cultural styles of the other. (For
example, is the White attraction to Black youth culture connected with Blacks
being seen as "bad," as oppositional, in a way that covertly reinforces the stigma-
tizing of Blacks in American life?)

4. In the three times I have taught the course, I have never had an East Asian student, though I have had several South Asians. Although there are five times as many Black students as Asians, this does not explain the racial gap in enrollment, as the Black group is always oversubscribed. I think that for many students at the high school, "race and racism" is a Black or possibly Black and White issue. Once a Black student said she was surprised that there were any White students in the class, and, she implied, any non-Black students at all.

5. At the same time, I should make clear that, while the reading material is very demanding, the work load is generally not as severe as in the students' AP classes, although it is more so than in their non-AP ones.

6. I did not directly challenge the stereotyping that emerged in the postclass interviews, since I was trying to allow the students to elaborate their own views and those of their families.

7. Many thanks to Meira Levinson, Rick Weissbourd, Martha Minow, and Mary Casey, and especially to Ben Blum-Smith, as well as the editors of *Radical Teacher*, for feedback on previous drafts of this chapter.

REFERENCES

Fordham, S., & Ogbu, J. U. (1986). "Black students' school success: Coping with the burden of acting White," *The Urban Review, 18*(3), 1–31.

Jencks, C., & Phillips, M. (Eds.). (1998). *The Black-White test score gap.* Washington, DC: Brookings Institution Press.

Lewin, T. (2002). Growing up, growing apart. In J. Lelyveld and correspondents of the *New York Times, How race is lived in America* (pp. 151–170). New York: MacMillan.

Oakes, J. (1985). *Keeping track: How schools structure inequality.* New Haven: Yale University Press.

Ogbu, J. U. (2002). *Black American students in an affluent suburb: A study of academic disengagement.* Mahwah, NJ: Lawrence Erlbaum.

Steele, C. M., & Aronson, J. (1998). Stereotype threat and the test performance of academically successful African Americans. In C. Jencks and M. Phillips (Eds.), *The Black-White test score gap.* Washington, DC: Brookings Institution Press.

Walker, T. (2002, Fall). "Something is wrong here": Denver students confront racial tracking at their high school. *Teaching Tolerance, 22.* Retrieved March 8, 2008, from www.tolerance.org/teach/printar.jsp?p=0&ar=321&pi=ttm

Wheelock, A. (1992). *Crossing the tracks: How "untracking" can save America's schools.* New York: New Press.

COURSE MATERIALS

The main text for the course is Audrey Smedley's *Race in North America: Origins and Evolution of a Worldview*, 2nd edition (Westview, 1999). I also use *The History of Mary Prince, a West Indian Slave* (1831) and selections from Ira Berlin's *Many Thousands Gone: The First Two Centuries of Slavery in North America* (Harvard University Press, 1998). Other selections are from David Walker, *Appeal to the Colored Citizens of the World* (1830); Benjamin Banneker's letter to Thomas Jefferson concerning Black intellectual capabilities; Nathan Huggins, *Black Odyssey*; Haney-Lopez, *White by Law: The Legal Construction of Race*; David Roediger, *Wages of Whiteness*; Joseph Lelyveld and New York Times staff, *How Race Is Lived in America: Pulling Together, Pulling Apart*; Garrod, et al., eds., *Souls Looking Back: Life Stories of Growing Up Black*; and Lisa Funderberg, ed., *Black/White/Other: Biracial Americans Talk about Race and Identity*.

CHAPTER 9

Naming and Interrogating
Our English-Only Legacy

Lilia I. Bartolomé and Pepi Leistyna

> Any man who comes here must adopt . . . the native tongue of
> our people. . . . It would be a crime . . . to perpetuate differences
> in language in this country.
> —Theodore Roosevelt

THESE WORDS, written more than a century ago, could easily be misperceived as being written today in support of English-only laws and mandates. A recent *Washington Post* headline reads, "Spanish at School Translates to Suspension"; the story is about a high school junior in Kansas City who was suspended for a day and a half for responding to a friend's request in the school hallway with, "No problema" (Reid, 2005).

States such as California, Arizona, and Massachusetts have ushered in modern-day versions of non-English-language prohibition. We refer to these English-only mandates as "modern-day prohibition" because if we examine history, we find that although there have been exceptional moments in time (the 1960s to the 1980s) when languages other than English have been tolerated in schools and other institutions, the practice of forbidding the use of non-English languages has constituted the more prevalent language practice in the United States.

What we are experiencing currently across the nation, as in the past, is what Terrence Wiley (1999) refers to as a veiled (and not so veiled) racist ideology, a "prevailing English-only ideology in the United States [which] not only positions English as the dominant language, but also presumes universal English monolingualism to be a natural and ideal condition. . . . [This] English monolingual ideology sees language diversity as a problem that is largely a consequence of immigration, and it equates the acquisition of English with assimilation, patriotism, and what it means to be an

American" (pp. 25–26). In order to comprehend the current xenophobic English-only movement, it is necessary to critically understand this nation's assimilationist and English monolingual legacy not only in terms of its application to past European immigrants but most importantly, for our discussion, also in terms of its application to indigenous and non-White linguistic minorities.

In addition to making this distinction, we contend that it is necessary to take a critical sociohistorical perspective in order to begin to do what noted critical pedagogue Paulo Freire (1985) encouraged educators to do when confronted with educational problems or obstacles faced by subordinated student populations. Freire argued that in order to solve an educational problem, it was necessary first to comprehensively and historically under-stand the problem—that is, to comprehensively "construct" the problem. The next step, after situating the problem historically, is to critically ana-lyze it—to "deconstruct" the issue. The third and final step is to imagine alternative possibilities, to realistically dream about implementing more humane democratic solutions—to "reconstruct" the problem and develop a solution. As radical educators, our aim is precisely that—to critically con-struct the current English-only, native-language prohibition state of affairs so as to deconstruct it and then reconstruct it, to come up with ways to better intellectually prepare and politically arm linguistic-minority students rather than set them up for academic failure and life on the margins of society.

TRACING THE COLONIAL LEGACY

As pointed out in the work of many of the early anticolonial theorists/ revolutionaries (see Fanon, 1967; Memmi, 1965), imperialists have always understood the relationship between knowledge and power and the cen-tral role of that relationship in controlling the psyche of people, in the arena of public opinion, and consequently in maintaining systems of oppression. They recognized how material conditions, politics, and culture are inter-laced and how subordination and opposition take place in both the physi-cal and symbolic realms. As such, colonizers and fascists alike immediately go after schools, media, and other public spheres that produce and dis-seminate knowledge.

The United States is no stranger to this colonizing philosophy and practice of cultural invasion. When we examine language policy in regards to domestic linguistic-minority groups such as Native Americans, Native Hawaiians, Mexican Americans in the Southwest, and descendents of enslaved Africans, we find that the sanctioned practice of linguistic sup-pression and cultural domestication has been the historical norm. One only has to examine the case of enslaved Africans, the first victims of repressive policies. Under the threat of brutal punishment, enslaved Africans were forbidden from speaking their native tongues and teaching them to their children. Furthermore, compulsory-illiteracy laws were passed in Southern colonies to prohibit slaves from learning to read or write. If we examine the legacy of Native Americans, we see that they too underwent horrific repressive policies that kept them separated from and subordinate to the White dominant culture. They were treated as dependent wards; had their lands taken away by Whites; and had their children forced into boarding schools, many of which were former military bases, and systematically stripped of their language and culture. Mexicans and Mexican Americans in the Southwest suffered similarly after the U.S. conquest of what used to be northwest Mexico.

This colonial legacy would feed into the English-only ideology that became hegemonic during World War I with the rise of the Americanization movement and the rampant persecution of speakers of German. However, in examining the origins of English-only ideologies, we must highlight the differences between the experiences of European immigrants such as those from Germany and Poland and non-White subordinated minorities. As Wiley (1999) explains, "Despite the severity of the attack on the German language and the persecution of German Americans during WWI, there was no systematic effort to segregate them from Anglo Americans, as was the case for language minorities of color in the years following WWI" (p. 28). This was certainly the case during World War II, when Japanese Americans were stripped of their property and interned while German Americans and Italian Americans were not. In fact, Asian Americans also have faced a long history of brutality in the United States.

According to Ronald Schmidt (as cited in Wiley, 1999), the experience of linguistic minorities of color has been noticeably different from that of European immigrants in several respects:

1. Non-White linguistic minorities were extended the benefits of public education more slowly and grudgingly than were European Americans despite the fact that they too were taxed for this.
2. When education was offered to non-White linguistic minorities, it was usually done in segregated and inferior schools.
3. Non-White linguistic-minority groups' cultures and languages were denigrated by public educators and others. In addition, these groups were denied the opportunity to maintain and perpetuate their cultural heritage through the public schools.
4. Reflective of these visible forms of rejection and exclusion by the dominant group in society, the education that was offered was

exclusively assimilationist and functioned not to integrate the groups into the dominant culture, but to subordinate and socialize them for second-class citizenship. (List taken and modified from Wiley, 1999, p. 28)[1]

It is important to reiterate that even though language policies aimed at European immigrants and non-White linguistic-minority groups can also be described as "assimilationist," in the case of non-Whites, they involved domestication rather than integration. Taking away the native tongue while never really giving access to the discourse of power is a common practice in any colonial model of education. Such a deskilling process, in which people are rendered semiliterate in both languages, effectively works to deny them access to the mainstream while simultaneously taking away essential tools that can be used to build the cultural solidarity necessary to resist exploitation and democratize and transform society. Donaldo Macedo, Bessie Dendrinos, and Panayota Gounari (2003) powerfully explain the distinctive and oppressive nature of what they call "colonial bilingualism":

> There is a radical difference between a dominant speaker learning a second language and a minority speaker acquiring a dominant language. While the former involves the addition of a second language to one's linguistic repertoire, the latter usually inflicts the experience of subordination upon the minority speaker—both when speaking his or her native language, which is devalued by the dominant culture, and when speaking the dominant language he or she has learned, often under coercive condition. Furthermore, the colonized's mother tongue, that which is sustained by his feelings, emotions, and dreams, that in which his tenderness and wonder are expressed, thus that which holds the greatest emotional impact, is precisely the one which is the least valued. . . . [The colonized] must bow to the language of his master (pp. 80–81).

Homi Bhabha's (1994) concept of "ambivalence" sheds light on how assimilation paradoxically works toward segregation and domestication rather than inclusion. In the operations of colonial discourses, Bhabha theorized a process of identity construction that was built on a constant ideological pulling by a central force from contrary directions in which the "other" (the colonized) is positioned as both alien and yet knowable, that is, deviant and yet able to be assimilated. To keep the colonial subject at a necessary distance—unable to participate in the rights of full citizenship—stereotypes are used to dehumanize the oppressed, while benevolence and kind gestures are superimposed to rehumanize them. To use a current example, Latino/as in the United States are represented as lazy, shiftless, violent, and unintelligent, dehumanized by the press as "illegal aliens" and "non-White hordes." The language of popular culture embraces more blatant racist language: "border rats," "wetbacks," "spics," and so on. These same people are simultaneously deemed worthy of a good education, standard language skills, employment, and advancement.[2] The oppressors are thus positioned as benign and beneficent so as to rhetorically rebut any criticism of their abuse. However, any simple deconstruction of the actual contradictory and debilitating practices that they endorse reveals the hypocrisy of these "good intentions."

The problem with providing a good education—one that produces youth who not only are fluent and literate, are well rounded in their knowledge of the world, and have a solid sense of history, but also are able to understand the relations of power that shape their lives and read into the values and beliefs that inform societal practices and their own actions—is that it nurtures a critical citizenry able to effectively participate in public life. Well-educated people can be a menace to those in power, as they have access to the cultural capital and strategies used by the colonizer to maintain the material and symbolic system of oppression. As John McLeod (2000) explains, "Hearing their language returning through the mouths of the colonized, the colonizers are faced with the worrying threat of resemblance between colonizer and colonized" (p. 55). These forces of resistance are able to effectively navigate both worlds and can work to transform the inhumane conditions that so many people are forced to live in on a daily basis. Hence the reason for simultaneously calling for a quality education for all (the U.S. English Foundation makes claims to disseminating "a vehicle of opportunity [English] for new Americans") while ensuring faulty pedagogical models and dysfunctional institutional policies, practices, and expectations. Referring to the British in colonial India, Bhabha describes this assimilationist trap: "To be Anglicized is emphatically not to be English" (p. 87). In the case of the United States, it is to be Americanized but never really accepted as American, and never granted the power to even influence such a definition, let alone achieve full participation in society.

THE PAST REARS ITS UGLY HEAD

Capitalizing on the public's general discontent with K–12 schools, proponents of English-only have worked tirelessly and effectively to scapegoat bilingual education, creating legal constraints on the daily lives of educators by ensuring that languages other than English (with the exception of those employed in "foreign-language instruction"—although some schools even want to ban these courses) are stomped out of school life entirely.

Antibilingual-education forces have also capitalized on public fears over national unity. The U.S. English Foundation (n.d.) believes that "a shared language provides a cultural guidepost that we must maintain for the sake of our country's unity, prosperity, and democracy." Not only does this dehistoricized position presuppose that the country has at some point been united, but its ideologues strategically say nothing about a system within which people are relegated, and not by choice, to live on the margins of linguistic, economic, social, and political power.

At the forefront of the most recent assault by the English-only movement is Ron Unz, the chairman of the national advocacy organization English for the Children and the originator of California's Proposition 227, which in 1998 effectively outlawed bilingual education in that state. After a similar victory in Arizona in 2000, he also attempted to win over Colorado. However, a wealthy parent spent a mountain of her own personal money on a press campaign to persuade the middle-class, voting, White majority not to support Unz's initiative, warning that if bilingual programs are dismantled then "those kids will be in class with your kids." This well-funded, racist plea worked and Colorado voted no on the English-only referendum. Nonetheless, after taking over Massachusetts in 2002, Unz focused in on New York and Oregon.

This monolingual business mogul, who has no children and no academic or experiential background with language acquisition, demands that the United States replace bilingual education—that is, grade-appropriate, native language instruction in the content areas while English proficiency is achieved—with a 1-year Structured English Immersion Program. As the English for the Children publicity pamphlet states:

> Under this learning technique, youngsters not fluent in English are placed in a separate classroom in which they are taught English over a period of several months. Once they have become fluent in English, they are moved into regular classes. (quoted in Leistyna, 2002, p. 214)

However, there is no defensible theory or body of research to support the claim that students need only 1 year (about 180 school days) to become fully fluent, literate, and able to learn content in another language and then face high-stakes standardized tests in that language. Imagine yourself going to another country where you didn't speak the language and pulling off this feat in such a short period of time. In Massachusetts, those students who do not pass the state's standardized test are not awarded a high school diploma. Instead, they are handed a certificate of attendance and shown the door.

Regardless of Unz's rhetorical claims, the majority of students in California in Structured English Immersion did not achieve even intermediate fluency after 1 year. Take, for example, the Orange Unified School District, which is so often used to support his argument: after the 1st year, 6 students out of 3,549 were mainstreamed; more than half the students were not ready for his specially designed classrooms. A more recent progress report in California reveals the extent of the disaster:

> In 2002–2003, it [Ron Unz's Structured English Immersion] failed at least 1,479,420 children who remained limited in English. Only 42 percent of California students whose English was limited in 1998, when Proposition 227 passed, have since been redesignated as fluent in English—five years later! (Crawford, 2003, p.1)

Given this utter failure, in this era of No Child Left Behind, we need to take a critical look at sheltered English instruction to understand the approach's possibilities and how it is being misused to ensure the failure of so many young people.

Early proponents of sheltered English instruction understood that academic language proficiency can take up to 7 years to acquire and that even affluent English-language learners require 5 to 8 years to score as well as native speakers on standardized tests (Collier, 1987). Stephen Krashen (1985) presented a detailed model for sheltered English that included the percentage of time students spent in three settings: (1) the mainstream English-only classroom, (2) the sheltered English classroom, and (3) the native language development classroom. David and Yvonne Freeman (1988) write: "In this model, beginning level students are mainstreamed with native English speaking peers initially in music, art, physical education—the subjects that are least linguistically demanding." In addition, the students study English as a second language in the sheltered English classroom while they study all core academic subjects in their first language so as not to fall behind academically while they learn English. When the students acquire intermediate-level English-language proficiency, additional academic subjects such as math and science are taught in sheltered English classrooms, while social studies and language arts continue to be taught in the students' first language. At the advanced level, remaining academic subjects—language arts and social studies—are taught in sheltered English classrooms, and the students are mainstreamed into "regular" English-only classes for all other courses. This type of sheltered English instruction was conceptualized to assist students in developing academic competence in the native language while also developing English proficiency in the sheltered classroom.

However, when we examine how sheltered English instruction is implemented in Massachusetts and other states that have mandated similar English-only laws, we can clearly see the corruption of Krashen's concept; his initial comprehensive and longitudinal approach was appropriated and perverted by English-only ideologues and translated to a 1- or 2-year English-only program of instruction with little regard for students' English-language proficiency levels in determining classroom placements. Furthermore, in some school systems students are segregated with little exposure to native English speakers or other more English-proficient peers and penalized if caught speaking a language other than English. These illogical and dysfunctional language programs are very effective at making sure that so many students remain uneducated and thus unable to fully participate in this democratic society.

Ironically, some antibilingual advocates (including the late former president Ronald Reagan) have insisted that instruction in languages other than English is un-American. This paradoxical twist disregards the fact that the Constitution of the United States protects linguistic pluralism and that the U.S. Supreme Court's 1974 *Lau v. Nichols* decision was intended to protect the rights of linguistic minorities in public schools. States like Alaska and Oklahoma found English-only practices in government to be unconstitutional. It also seems quite unpatriotic for a democracy to exclude (or mark as "foreign") languages that are now indigenous to the United States: the native tongues of Puerto Rico, Native America, and Hawaii and those of African Americans and Mexican Americans.

What is particularly disturbing is that the national "debates" over bilingual education have very little to do with language acquisition. The media and the general public seem much more inclined to talk about the people who speak particular languages than about the languages that they speak and how they are learned. As witnessed in the controversy over using Ebonics in public schools, the mainstream discourse has focused on images of African Americans rather than the historical, cultural, and linguistic developments of Black English(es). The popular debates thus have more to do with dominant representations of the pros and cons of particular groups, especially Blacks and Latino/as. Such a focus not only disregards the multiplicity of other linguistically diverse groups that are at the mercy of powerful antibilingual proponents, but it also reveals what is in fact a racialized debate. For example, the English for the Children publicity pamphlet poses the question, "What is 'bilingual education'?" To which it eagerly responds,

> Although "bilingual education" may mean many things in theory, in the overwhelming majority of American schools, "bilingual

education" is actually Spanish-almost-only instruction. (quoted in Leistyna, 2002, p. 222)

The word *Spanish* is often strategically used as a code word for the largest, and a demographically growing, political force in the country—Latino/a groups. This racialized marker creates fear among Whites that English-only advocates not only perpetuate, but play off of. There is a not so subtle play on public fears that the "unwashed brown masses" from impoverished countries like Mexico and Haiti are on their way to the States. In a cover story in *Commentary*, with the shock value title of "California and the End of White America," Unz (1999) is able to sustain the existing and balkanizing fear in many Whites that they are being overrun, while at the same time scaring racially and ethnically diverse peoples with the "inevitability" that there will be White backlash against them in the form of "White Nationalism." He warns:

> Our political leaders should approach these ethnic issues by reaffirming America's traditional support for immigration, but couple that with a return to the assimilative policies which America has emphasized in the past. Otherwise, whites as a group will inevitably begin to display the same ethnic-minority-group politics as other minority groups, and this could break our nation. We face the choice of either supporting "the New American Melting Pot" or accepting "the Coming of White Nationalism" (p. 1).

Unz's own racism, and his embodiment of Bhabha's notion of ambivalence, can be clearly witnessed in his comment to the *Los Angeles Times* (1997) when he said of his Jewish grandparents, who were poor and immigrated to California in the 1920s and 1930s: "They came to WORK and become successful . . . not to sit back and be a burden on those who were already here!" (p. 1).

Not surprisingly, antibilingual proponents tell the public virtually nothing about the horrific material and symbolic conditions that so many children and young adults face in schools that reflect the larger social order. The reality is that 75% of all linguistic-minority students reside in low-income, urban areas. These students often face harsh racist attitudes, crumbling buildings, incessant harassment, segregated school activities, limited classroom materials, ill-prepared teachers, poorly designed and unenforced policies, and indifferent leadership that dramatically disrupt their personal, cultural, and academic lives.[3] Within this climate, the appalling conditions faced by both bilingual and English as a second language teachers and their children are by no means conducive to assimilation, let alone selective acculturation, and, by no stretch of the imagination, to social transformation.

When poverty is acknowledged by English-only advocates, bilingual education is identified as one of the culprits. Unz states that bilingual education is a place where children "remain imprisoned" and thus is about "guaranteeing that few would ever gain the proficiency in English they need to get ahead in America" (quoted in Leistyna, 2002, p. 221). The English for the Children pamphlet adds, "Children who leave school without knowing how to read English, write English, and speak English are injured for life economically and socially" (quoted in Leistyna, 2002, p. 221). Unz neglects to recognize the fact that even in the cases where English is one's primary language, this does not guarantee economic, political, and integrative success. For example, Native Americans, Native Hawaiians, Chicano/as, and African Americans have been speaking English for generations in this country, and yet the majority of the members of these groups still remain socially, economically, and politically subordinated. The proportion of racially subordinated workers earning low wages in 2003 is substantial—30.4% of Black workers and 39.8% of Latino/a workers (Economic Policy Institute, 2004/2005). The median income of racially subordinated families is $25,700, as compared with $45,200 for White families (Dollars & Sense and United for a Fair Economy, 2004). A consistent pattern in the data has shown that the unemployment rate for African Americans and Latino/as over the years has remained more than double that of Whites. While about 10% of White children live in poverty in the United States, more than 30% of African American and Latino/a kids experience harsh economic conditions.

The same racialized economic hardship falls on migrant workers and immigrants. Beyond the concocted hype about the usurping of quality employment by "outsiders," the job opportunities that are intended for this sector of the labor force consist of low-wage manual labor: on cleaning crews, in food service, under the monotony of the assembly line, and in farmwork. A system of poor education and restrictive language and literacy practices ensure reproduction of the cheap and exploitable labor force.

Thus, the issue isn't simply about language. White supremacy, classism, and the logic of capital, as well as other kinds of structural inequities and discrimination, play a much larger role in limiting one's access to social, economic, institutional, and legal power.

Instead of seriously addressing such issues, the English-only coalition serves up myths of meritocracy and life in a melting pot where the patterns of a "common culture" and economic success miraculously emerge if one is willing to submit to their agenda.[4]

It is important to note here that so many mainstream politicians concerned with public education work so hard to eradicate multilingualism among racially and economically oppressed students, while simultaneously working to make certain that upper-middle-class and wealthy youth—their own kids—are multilingual. Multilingualism, which is embraced in all the finest private schools in the country, and worldwide, for that matter, is great for elite children but somehow bad for, and unpatriotic on the part of, the non-White and poor.

TAKING A RADICAL STAND

Although current English-only mandates are presented in ways that render them "kinder and gentler" (as epitomized by the slogan "English for the Children") than the blatant intolerant, nativist language policies of the past, the fact is that linguistic-minority students remain tongue-tied in their native language. One significant characteristic of present-day English-only language policy is that it is official language policy rather than the unofficial array of policies of the past. In addition, in states such as Massachusetts, one particular pedagogical approach—sheltered English—is being dictated to school districts.

Advocates of linguistic-minority students, in particular bilingual teachers, need to resist being cowed into submission by these new English-only laws and mandates for sheltered English instruction as the sole vehicle for language and literacy development in classrooms. Despite the bleak conditions imposed by English-only ideologues, the power of teachers' political clarity and authentic commitment to linguistic-minority students can serve to work to their advantage and success.

As bilingual/ESL teachers and advocates for linguistic-minority students, we must not forget that our work with these students—most of whom are not White and come from low socioeconomic status groups—is a political and ideological undertaking. We seemed to forget this fact when bilingual-education advocates, under attack, presented bilingual education as a technical issue and defended it with arguments based solely on research findings and statistics. Unfortunately, we tended to view and treat bilingual education as strictly a pedagogical issue and shied away from its political and ideological dimensions. Of course, now we realize that our work is highly political and ideological and that it doesn't boil down to finding the right or magical methods to effectively teach our students. Fundamentally, our arguments should be rooted in human and civil rights, much in the way that they were in the 1960s and 1970s.

We have much to learn from the courage and tenacity of one former bilingual teacher in California who perceives that state's English-only mandate (Proposition 227) as a temporary obstacle that can eventually be overcome:

> Proposition 227 really pushed people that [believed in bilingual education] to [continue fighting] for our dream. It's like a soccer game. You didn't make the goal. Oh well . . . you have the chance [to get up and try] again. Soccer players fall many times during a game. They trip over each other. We can trip over these policies and fall over these laws . . . but I'm going to get up again. I'll keep going. When things like Proposition 227 happen, don't trip, fall, and stay [lying] down. (quoted in Stritikus & Garcia, 2003, p. 25)

This teacher's powerful words remind us that we must always get up to protect our children and to demand that they be treated with the dignity and respect they deserve.

As we can see from an historical overview of language education in this country, the domestication and subordination that are essential to any colonial model are still very much present in English-only ideology and school practices. Instead of uncritically neutralizing the potential of multilingual programs, the public needs to explore what ensures that such undertakings don't succeed and why. The debate over bilingual education shouldn't be left in the hands of a savvy politician who is strategically vying for popular clout through theoretical ambiguities and representational manipulations of what's best for children. Instead, educators need to work tirelessly to get substantive information out to the public, even touting its effectiveness to those members of the dominant culture who may be sincerely concerned with language policy and practice but have temporarily fallen prey to manipulative and malicious ideologies—so that people can in turn protect themselves and their children when ignorance and deceit come, and they will, to your state.

NOTES

1. This physical and symbolic violence has continued through the years. Patricia MacGregor-Mendoza (2000) reports the memories of New Mexican adults who shared their own experiences in schools with "unofficial" yet enforced English-only school policies. One woman recounted: "If we tried to speak Spanish, our teachers would tell us, 'Speak English dammit, this is America.' Well, one day, don't think I got fed up with it, and I told her, 'You're the one in my country, you should learn my language.' You should of seen her face, she got so angry. She went to pick up a ruler and she hit me in the face with it" (unedited student writing).

Aida Hurtado and Raul Rodriguez (1989) share similar research findings. They report that more than 40% of 500 Spanish-speaking Texas college students they interviewed reported having experienced some form of recrimination for speaking Spanish while attending primary or secondary school.

2. As an essential part of this process of maintaining ambivalence, colonizers need members of the subordinated classes who can speak the dominant tongue and express all its uses and beliefs as superior and benevolent "gifts." This is exemplified in the United States in the work of such public figures as Richard Rodriguez and Jaime Escalante, who served as the honorary chairman of Proposition 227. Bhabha (1994) refers to these agents as "mimic men."

3. Unz disregards these political and ethical issues and simply calls for "structured mixing," when possible, of mainstream and Structured English Immersion students. Not only does his plan avoid confronting the discrimination that takes place in public educational institutions—that in fact leads to high drop-out rates—but it is also unclear how such a strategy for integration is going to work in schools that are segregated because of economic/housing demographics.

4. Unz (2000), a self-professed opponent of bilingual education, affirmative action, multiculturalism, and multicultural education, insists: "First and foremost, our public schools and educational instruction must be restored as the engines of assimilation they once were. . . . In history and social studies classrooms, 'multicultural education' is now widespread, placing an extreme and unrealistic emphasis on ethnic diversity instead of passing on the traditional knowledge of Western civilization, our Founding Fathers, and the Civil and World Wars. . . . Current public school curricula which glorify obscure ethnic figures at the expense of the giants of American history have no place in a melting pot framework" (pp. 3–4).

REFERENCES

Bhabha, H. (1994). *The location of culture*. New York: Routledge.

Collier, V. (1987). Age and rate of acquisition of second language for academic purposes. *TESOL Quarterly, 21,* 617–641.

Crawford, J. (2003). A few things Ron Unz would prefer you didn't know about English learners in California. Retrieved March 8, 2008, from http://lourworld.compuserve.com/homepages/JWCRAWFORD/castats.htm

Crawford, J. (2004). *Educating English learners: Language diversity in the classroom.* Los Angeles: Bilingual Educational Services.

Dollars & Sense and United for a Fair Economy. (Eds.). (2004). *The wealth and inequality reader.* Cambridge, MA: Economic Affairs Bureau.

Economic Policy Institute. (2004/2005). *The state of working America.* Ithaca, NY: ILR Press.

Fanon, F. (1967). *Black skin, white masks.* New York. Grove Press.

Freeman, D., & Freeman, Y. (1988). Sheltered English instruction. *ERIC Digest.* ERIC Document Reproduction Service No. ED301070.

Freire, P. (1985). *The politics of education: Culture, power, and liberation.* New York: Bergin & Garvey.

Hurtado, A., & Rodriguez, R. (1989). Language as a social problem: The repression of Spanish in South Texas. *Journal of Multilingual and Multicultural Development, 10*(5), 401–419.

Krashen, S. (1985). *Insights and inquiries.* Hayward, CA: Alemany Press.

Leistyna, P. (2002). Scapegoating bilingual education: Getting the whole story from the trenches. *Bilingual Research Journal, 26*(2), 213–239.

Macedo, D., Dendrinos, B., & Gounari, P. (2003). *The hegemony of English.* Boulder, CO: Paradigm.

MacGregor-Mendoza, P. (2000). No se habla Español: Stories of linguistic repression in Southwest schools. *Bilingual Research Journal, 24*(4), 355–367.

McLeod, J. (2000). *Beginning postcolonialism.* Manchester: Manchester University Press.

Memmi, A. (1965). *The colonizer and the colonized.* Boston: Beacon Press.

Reid, T. R. (2005, December 9). Spanish at school translates to suspension. *The Washington Post,* p. A03.

Stritikus, T., & Garcia, E. (2003, August 6). The role of theory and policy in the educational treatment of language minority students: Competitive structures in California. *Education Policy Analysis Archives, 11*(26), 1–31. Retrieved March 4, 2004, from http://epaa.ast.edulepass/vl1n26/.

Unz, R. (1997, August 31). As cited in M. Barabak, GOP bid to mend rift with Latinos still strained. *The Los Angeles Times.*

Unz, R. (1999, November). California and the end of White America. *Commentary.* Retrieved March 1, 2004, from http://www.onena-tion.orgI9911/110199 .html

Unz, R. (2000, April/May). The right way for Republicans to handle ethnicity in politics. *American Enterprise.* Retrieved March 1, 2004, from www.onenation .org0004/0400.html

U.S. English Foundation. (n.d.). *Welcome to U.S. English Foundation.* Retrieved March 8, 2008, from http://www.usefoundation.org/foundation/

Wiley, T. G. (1999). Comparative historical analysis of U.S. language policy and language planning: Extending the foundations. In T. Huebner & K. Davies (Eds.), *Sociopolitical perspectives on language policy and planning in the US* (pp. 17–38). Philadelphia: Benjamin.

PART IV

Teaching About Gender and Sexualities

Teaching and Learning Through Desire, Crisis, and Difference: Perverted Reflections on Anti-oppressive Education

Kevin K. Kumashiro

WHEN I THINK about the concerns currently expressed by my student teachers, I hear the repetition of at least two sets of questions that my colleagues and I grappled with when I was a schoolteacher a few years ago. One, how do we motivate students to study, to think, to ask; in other words, how do we foster in students a desire to learn? Two, how do we teach uncomfortable and controversial material without upsetting students, parents, and community members; in other words, how do we avoid crisis? As reflected in numerous educational journals and books, video documentaries, and teacher certification courses, these questions play a central role in contemporary educational inquiry and practice. However, these questions do not necessarily go hand in hand with a form of education that actively and intentionally works against oppression (i.e., education that changes racism, sexism, heterosexism, etc.), what I call "anti-oppressive" education. In fact, my own teaching experiences suggest to me that these questions, with their commonsense or normalized notions of "desire" and "crisis," make possible only certain ways of thinking about and engaging in anti-oppressive education, and make impossible or unimaginable other, and perhaps more effective, approaches to teaching and learning against oppression.

In what follows, I reflect on my experiences teaching high school students and student teachers and argue that teaching was made meaningful, and learning against oppression was made possible, only when we —consciously or unconsciously—made use of nonnormalized or perverted forms of desire and crisis. My language here is intentional: Reflections on the "perverted" involve not only a deviation from what is commonly considered good, right, or true in education, but also an incorporation of the "queer" into practices that often cling to the norm, as I will explain later on. Throughout the essay, I include statements that some of my students have expressed orally and in writing to each other and to me as I attempt to represent some of the troubling conversations I hear in education.

FROM DESIRING RATIONALITY TO ENTERING CRISIS

Three years ago, I taught a 2-week workshop in a summer program for high school students of color. Of the seven afternoon workshops, my workshop was the only one that focused explicitly on oppression (in particular, on racist, sexist, and heterosexist stereotypes). All my students had chosen to be in my workshop, which suggests to me that they desired to engage in anti-oppressive education. I, too, desired to engage in anti-oppressive education, and drawing on such theorists as Paulo Freire (1970), and Henry Giroux and Peter McLaren (1989), I envisioned my role as that of a "critical" educator, one who helps students to "critique and transform" oppressive social structures and ideologies. According to my syllabus, we were to do this rationally: The 1st week would be spent learning about the dynamics of oppression (as we examine a range of stereotypes and answer the question "Why are stereotypes harmful?"), and the 2nd week would be spent acting on this knowledge as we engaged in an activist project.

As the 1st week came to an end, my students' and my own reliance on rational learning and teaching brought us to a stuck place (I explain this in more depth in Kumashiro, 1999). For my students, learning about oppression exceeded the realm of the rational and abstract. Their participation could not remain at the level of intellectual and detached conversation and debates about "what are the stereotypes of this group?" or "why are these stereotypes harmful to them?" Rather, they seemed to be confronting their own emotions and life experiences and, in the process, entering a form of "crisis." They became upset, saying they felt "bad" or "guilty" as they recounted times when they stereotyped others and were themselves stereotyped and yet had not been aware that this was happening because they had not considered such occurrences to be abnormal. As they learned about the dynamics of oppression, they were unlearning what they previously had learned was "normal," was not harmful, was just the way things are. And, as they unlearned what was "normal" and normative (i.e., the way things ought to be), they were learning about their own privileges and complicities with oppression, such as ways they were privileged by heterosexism, or ways they bought into, and thus contributed to, a racial hierarchy in which, say, Latinas were sexualized, Black men were dehumanized, and Asian Americans were considered unharmed by racism. Having learned about their own role in oppression, they now needed a way to feel better about themselves. Thus, we were "stuck," unable to move on with the more academic parts of the lesson because I had not incorporated into my lesson plan a way to address this emotional crisis.

Yet, as Shoshana Felman (1995) suggests, educators should expect students to enter crisis. In fact, she argues that "teaching in itself, teaching as such, takes place precisely only through crisis" (p. 55). How so? Consider the difference between education and repetition. "Education" is not about repeating what we already know, or affirming what we already believe, or reinforcing what we previously learned. That is merely repetition. Education is about learning something new, something different; education is about change. Perhaps this is all common sense, but what is significant, here, is the recognition that repetition, such as the affirmation of who we are and what we believe, is often a comforting process, because it tells us that we are smart or good. In contrast, education—especially the process of learning something that tells us that the very ways in which we think and do things is not only wrong but also harmful—can be a very discomforting process. Hence the notion that learning takes place "only through crisis." Educators should expect their students to enter crisis. And, since this crisis can lead in one of many directions—such as toward liberating change, or toward more entrenched resistance—educators need to provide a space in the curriculum for students to work through their crisis in a way that changes oppression. Elsewhere (Kumashiro, 1999) I describe this process of working through crisis in more detail.

By realizing that anti-oppressive education necessarily involves crisis and getting stuck, educators can change the problematic ways in which their approaches to teaching and learning privilege rationality. For students, the desire to learn cannot be a desire to move forward rationally, that is to learn things that do not force the student to look within, to look back, to disrupt one's memories, to contradict one's worldview. Rather, the desire to learn must involve a desire to unlearn, a desire to return to what has already been learned, not to repeat or relearn it, but to unlearn it, to understand it in a different way, and to work through the resulting crisis.

Similarly, for teachers, the desire to teach cannot involve the facade of detachment. My students needed not an abstracted conversation about what they were going through, but a therapeutic activity in which they could work through their crisis. Leading such an activity required that I not be detached, impersonal, objective. Like my students, I needed to put myself into the lesson, to be attached, to listen to them, to share my own stories, and to address their needs. I needed to, and eventually did, rework my lesson plan and open a curricular space for my students to discuss their feelings and decide for themselves how they wanted to proceed with the lesson, which they did by writing and performing a skit for the other students in the program. They opened the skit by saying:

> Welcome! You are all gathered here for our group's play which is based on stereotypes, which was the focus of our workshop. Our play is called *Just Think*, which is something we all should do more often. Our play contains stereotypes, a lot of them, which may possibly offend some people but are not meant to. Please pay attention, enjoy, and think while viewing our play! Thank you!!

And they concluded by saying:

> We're feeling bad about what we did—that's why we're doing this [skit]. We're not trying to lecture you; we're trying to share what we learned.

By owning up to their prior complicity with stereotyping, and by critiquing the power of stereotypes to harm, the students, through the skit, were able to work through their crisis (and do something activist in the process). It is significant to note that, although my original lesson plan called for my students to do an "activist project," it did not leave open the space for them to work through emotional crisis while doing so.

Even well-intentioned pedagogies, then, can be problematic. Ironically, such pedagogies can further marginalize the very students they intend to liberate. Critiquing "critical" educators (like the ones who initially influenced my lesson planning), Elizabeth Ellsworth (1992) tells us that the reliance on rationality and assumption of detachment really privilege the "mythical norm" (White American, male, etc.), serving as "repressive myths that perpetuate relations of domination." In my own class, I believe that my initial privileging of rationality harmed my students because it could not account for the excesses of emotion. In particular, the life experiences of my students of color, especially with racism, brought a historical and personal connection to the lessons on oppression that those who fit the mythical norm do not typically have; they had difficulty separating their heart from their mind when "understanding" racism. Their personal experiences as people not privileged on the basis of race exceeded the expectations of a pedagogy that relied on rationality and that repressed other ways of knowing and relating. I should note that even the ways my students were privileged required occasional departures from my lesson plan, such as when discussions of heterosexism and homophobia confronted a student with her own homophobia because they rubbed against and complicated memories of her favorite uncle, who happened to be gay. More than just acknowledging her privilege, this student wrestled with her privilege in a way that forced her to recognize parallels between heterosexual privilege and racial privilege and to see the benefits both (unfairly) bestow on different dominant groups in society. Because my lesson plan could not address these emotional and unpredicted events, it missed my students, Othering them because they could not be engaged by a pedagogy that presumed to address the mythical norm.

Deborah Britzman (1998b) suggests that this should not be surprising: Pedagogy's privileging of rationality and repressing of other ways of knowing and relating, such as "touching," is its defense mechanism against what it cannot control or predict. And, like the ego's defense mechanisms, pedagogy's privileging of rationality harms itself, works against its own goals, and, as in my case, leads to stuck places that it cannot work through, and that, instead, it constantly tries to avoid or foreclose. Yet, as I argued earlier, when teaching and learning against oppression occurs, crises cannot be avoided, should not be avoided, and must be worked through. This is not to say that rationality should be avoided. Rather, rationality must not be treated as the panacea, as the solution to our problems. While a rational pedagogy does make some teaching and learning possible, it can make other teaching and learning impossible. The desire to teach, then, especially the desire to teach students outside the mythical norm, cannot revolve solely around the desire to reason; it must also involve a desire to attach and touch, a desire to enter stuck and uncontrollable places, and a desire for crisis.

FROM DESIRING SAMENESS TO DESIRING CRISIS

I found myself in a different class entering a similarly stuck place last year when teaching a semester-long course on the relationship between school and society at a large midwestern university. This introductory-level course consisted of more than 30 undergraduate students, mostly White American, heterosexual women, most of whom were working toward certification in the teacher education program. We spent the first few weeks of the semester examining the paradoxical nature of schools that strive to give students equal educational opportunity but function to maintain various social hierarchies. As we discussed examples and theories of how and how often this happens, my students seemed to move, at least in their discussions, from feeling surprised, to critically reflecting on their own schooling experiences, to strategizing ways to address the problem. For this reason, I believe my students honestly desired to engage in anti-oppressive education. I, too, desired to engage in anti-oppressive education, wanting my students to think about schooling more critically and myself to teach more critically.

Although I did not realize it at the time, both desires, while perhaps well intentioned, revolved around affirming the self and remaining the same. For my students, the desire to learn involved learning only that which did not confront them with their own complicity with oppression. One student felt that schools are not responsible for social change and, instead, should follow the course set by others in society:

> I don't think that schools are responsible to initiate change. I think that artists, writers, lobbyists, activists, performers, the news media, thinkers of all types, spiritual leaders and political leaders are all responsible to initiate the social change attitude. Education can then take it from there.

Another student felt that teaching in ways that address oppression would detract from what schools were supposed to focus on, namely, academics:

> All the approaches deal so much with integrating racism, classism, sexism, and heterosexism into the curriculum, but will this take away from the true intention of schools to teach children academics?

Some students also felt that teachers should be morally neutral. As one put it:

> There are only 8 hours in a standard school day. If cultures, races, sexual orientations, etc., are going to be added to the curriculum, what is going to be taken out of the present system? The school day is already jam-packed with the basic classes. How can a curriculum incorporate all ideas and still leave room for math and science? Will not it seem like teachers are teaching their values on different ideas to their students?

One student felt that teachers are not part of the problem:

> I don't think that I have ever experienced a situation when students were directly oppressed by teachers in any way. The teachers were there to teach, not to impregnate their own beliefs or biases upon the students.

Many of my students acknowledged and condemned the ways schools perpetuate, say, racism, but asserted that, as teachers, their job will be to teach academics, not disrupt racism. They separated the school's function from the individual teacher's role, remaining secure in their belief that they do not—and, as future teachers, will not—contribute to these problems (J. Lei, personal communication, March 1999).

Some felt that teachers could blend antiracist teaching with academics through a "multicultural" curriculum, but only one in which students learn about different cultures, not about their own privileges, that is, about themselves. They did not believe their privileges made a difference in their education, and instead shifted the focus of our conversations to the people who were different from the norm at their school. As several students kept repeating in class discussions and in their final projects, if people can learn about different groups, and develop empathy for them, then ignorance, and the prejudice based on it, will be effectively combated. For example, students who felt they were becoming more "open-minded about homosexuals" talked about realizing that there is "nothing wrong" with them, that they are just like the norm (or the normal folks), and that they hurt just like everyone else. Learning, in this sense, was less an entry into difference, and more an affirmation of the self:

> I started the semester much more close-minded about the issue of homosexuality. After hearing many stories and reading the class materials, I finally have come to realize that there is nothing wrong with homosexuality. I think it helped that I got to know Kevin before he told us his sexuality, by that time it did not matter if he was gay or not.[1]

Not surprisingly, one student said:

> This article made me sad. I had an uncle who was gay. I realize that he wasn't treated equal when he was in school. He was one of the greatest guys I ever knew. He died last year, so it really hurt me to know that other gay people are experiencing what he had to experience.

The expectation that information about the Other leads to empathy is often based on the assumption that learning about "them" helps students see that "they" are like "us" (Britzman, 1998a). In other words, learning about the Other helps students see the self in the Other and thus does not change how they see themselves.

Similarly, my desire to teach involved teaching in ways that affirmed my knowledge and projected myself onto others. As I imagine many teachers do, I had planned lessons thinking that I knew (1) what my students knew and felt, (2) how I wanted my students to end up thinking and acting, and (3) what I needed to do in the lesson to get them to that place. Furthermore, in choosing their reading and writing assignments and planning the lessons, I had wanted my students to become at least somewhat like me, to think about schools and oppression critically (the way I think), to teach subversively (the way I teach). I soon learned, however, that anti-oppressive education cannot revolve around affirmation and sameness.

As my students and I moved to the section of the course on how teachers and schools might address the ways they function to maintain social hierarchies, I had them read an essay I wrote (an earlier draft of Kumashiro, 2000) that described four approaches to anti-oppressive education, and I had planned an activity to generate discussion around these four approaches. In terms of the three areas described above, I had assumed that they (1) knew little about addressing oppression in schools but were committed to doing so; (2) could implement the four approaches if they learned them; and, therefore, (3) should read about and discuss them in depth. However, when the class period began, we almost immediately got stuck at my use of the term *queer*.[2] One student said:

> You use the term *queer* throughout the article and it struck me as derogatory and actually really upset me until you clarified why you used it on page 11. As a suggestion, maybe you should explain how you use the term *queer* for a feeling of "self-empowerment" at the beginning. It would make the reader feel more comfortable. The more I think about it, maybe you should not use the term at all. I don't really think it's appropriate for this type of paper. I know that I personally cringed every time I read it.

Another said:

> Really don't like the word *queer*. I understand better why you chose the word *queer* but it's still a bit much [when said] over and over again—it just has a negative feel to it.

I had hoped to discuss the ways that students from traditionally marginalized groups in society are Othered in schools, but in a conversation where even some of the normally quiet students were speaking, many kept expressing feelings of discomfort and even anger at my use of a term that often meant something derogatory. Although I neglected before assigning the paper to discuss the history of the term *queer*, I did explain in the essay that *queer* has been claimed and appropriated by many queers to signify a conscious disassociation from normative sexuality and a sense of self-empowerment. Nonetheless, many were offended that I used a term that they had learned was politically correct to avoid. What they kept repeating in the discussion was the notion that *queer* meant something negative, and that I should instead use *homosexual* or *gay*, since those terms would not upset the (presumably) predominantly straight readership of the journal in which I was hoping to publish the paper.

I believe there are two main reasons why we were stuck on *queer*. One, it made explicit the constructedness and harmfulness of normalcy (i.e., how what is defined as "normal" is often normative in nature) and, in doing so, confronted my students with the discomforting process of disidentifying themselves with normalcy. The fluidity of sexuality signified by *queer* suggests that one's own sexual orientation is not fixed or given or natural, and thus it forces one to denaturalize one's own identity. Two, it invoked a history of ignorance, bigotry, and hatred and, in doing so, confronted my students with their own role and complicity in that history (L. Loutzenheiser, personal communication, March 1999). The preferred terms *homosexual* and *gay* do not stir up such a history. In fact, the medically pathologizing history of *homosexual* and the assimilationist history of *gay* (Tierney & Dilley, 1998) perhaps make it easier to disclaim heterosexism/homophobia as a viable form of oppression. Indeed, several students asserted that they did not believe that heterosexism/homophobia was as much of a problem as racism, classism, and sexism, which were the other forms of oppression addressed in the essay:

> I saw the title about anti-oppressive education, but the majority[3] of the examples used to explain the approaches dealt with homosexuality. I do not see homosexuality as the main problem. I would find it more helpful if more oppressive topics were discussed.

The hate-filled history of the term *queer* makes explicit the existence of heterosexism and homophobia, the severity of heterosexism/homophobia, and—if the student had ever used the term in a harmful way (or failed to intervene in such a situation)—the participation of the student in heterosexism/homophobia. So although my students did desire to learn, their desire for normalcy and for affirmation of their belief that they do not oppress others was stronger, preventing many of them from confronting and tolerating these new, discomforting forms of knowledge. In desiring to remain normal, they desired a repetition of the silence that normally surrounds heterosexism/homophobia, including their complicity with it, and thus entered a crisis when they met *queer*.

Our getting stuck on the term *queer* was also a crisis for me. I was completely surprised by their emotional reaction to my piece and unprepared for the resulting conversation. More important, I was upset not merely for being unprepared, but for being unprepared because I had fallen back on old habits. In the first place, yet again, I had planned a lesson that proceeded rationally: first, summarize the essay; second, extend the theories in the essay to other forms of oppression (since the essay focused on only four types of oppression). In other words, part of the problem was my failure to incorporate what I had learned from teaching the high schoolers 2 years earlier; I proceeded rationally and left little space for uncertainty and for working through crisis. In the second place, I yet again presumed to know my students when I did not. I expected to know how they would respond to my essay. In particular, while I did anticipate a crisis, I was expecting a different kind of crisis, one based on learning about the many ways oppression played out in their schooling years, not one based on resisting the very theories being presented. Clearly, the students were not whom I thought I was addressing.

Elizabeth Ellsworth (1997) tells us this is not surprising. Educators can never fully know our students. In addition, our students are all different from one another, and they all have multiple identities. An approach that assumes we can know students and can expect students to be a unitary audience will always miss them. And that is what happened. My lesson plan missed many of my students.

There were, of course, a few students who expressed support for my use of the term *queer*, and who thought of their experience reading the essay as a positive educational experience. One said:

> Upon reading the essay, I felt very happy. For once, I was reading an essay that dealt directly with the topic of discrimination in schools (especially with homosexuality).

Another student even felt the essay and its queerness was educationally useful:

> Personally, I had no problem with the use of the word *queer*. I was not offended by the word. I was actually intrigued to read on and find out what the actual meaning of the word *queer* is.

Another said:

> This is a voice that I've never heard before. This brought a whole
> new dimension to my frame of thinking. I'm not sure what it is but
> information like this gets my mind going. It has been true for me
> that when I had to work through a crisis, I grew and gained from
> the experience like no other time in my life. This is what life's all
> about for me: learning.

One student told me that she did not initially understand why I was
using *queer*, but reasoned that the discomfort she felt was perhaps part of
the learning process of reading my essay. She said that she wanted to learn,
which for her meant learning something new, hearing a different voice,
imagining the yet-unarticulated, doing the "unexpected." She preferred
learning things that made her uncomfortable and complicated her "frame
of thinking." In other words, her openness to my essay resulted from a
desire to learn that involved not a desire for affirmation and repetition,
but a desire for crisis and difference.

As the class discussion ensued, I encouraged my students to enter into
discomforting places and to think of learning as taking place only through
crisis. Modeling my own advice, I forced myself to enter an uncomfortable
place, departing from my lesson plan and teaching the unpredicted. Such a
move, I should note, is very difficult for me, as it is for many teachers who
desire control over the direction of the lesson and over what students learn.
Patti Lather (1998) tells us that educators often try to avoid crises and stuck
places in order to maintain a sense of control over what students learn (and,
for that matter, over how they behave). Yet, as my experiences show, we
can never control what students learn. It is only when educators acknowledge the impossibilities, unknowabilities, and uncontrollabilities of teaching, and work within stuck places, that change is possible. Thus, teaching
and learning against oppression cannot revolve around the desires for affirmation and sameness; students and teachers alike must be open to entering crisis and following the discomforting desire for difference.

Not until the end of the period did we discuss the four approaches. In
retrospect, not expecting to address crisis not only led me to plan a lesson
that could not be "achieved," but also, had I not departed from it, could
have prevented me from working with my students where they were at.
More and more, I am seeing that the goal of education needs to be change,
that is, getting students to a different place, out from repetition. This is
not to say that they should get to "where I am." I cannot foretell where
they (are to) go. And this is not to say that they should just go anywhere.

Where they go could be as (or even more) harmful than before. The goal, then, needs to be a change informed by theories of anti-oppressive education, a change that works against multiple forms of oppression. Embracing difference, refusing complicity, troubling privilege, engaging in activism —I believe these are changes in the right direction. In my class, I can never fully know how I affected my students. But I can at least take comfort in knowing that the resulting discussion in our classroom gave us a space to begin to work through our own individual crises and get unstuck.

I have tried to argue here that education involves many desires and crises, and that traditional and even well-intentioned approaches to teaching and learning do not always allow for the (perverted) desires and crises that can help students and teachers to work against oppression. As educators and educational researchers continue to unmask the roles that our various desires can and do play in teaching and learning, we should also ask what differences are made possible when we confront various forms of crisis through anti-oppressive education, and what it might look like when we do this. Now, when I teach, I begin the semester by making explicit my expectations that we often desire repetition, that differences can be upsetting, and that, consequently, learning takes place "only through crisis." It is not the panacea, but such an approach has allowed me to engage students in conversations where they seem interested in learning about oppression, open to confronting their own privileges and complicities, and better prepared to address the emotions and discomfort that come in the process.

NOTES

An earlier version of this chapter was presented at the Reclaiming Voice II Conference, held June 4 to 5, 1999, in Irvine, California. Thanks to Elizabeth Ellsworth, Lisa Loutzenheiser, Joy Lei, and especially my students for helping me think through the ideas in this paper.

1. I should note that I came out to my class as "bisexual" and "queer," not "gay." Yet, most students (and people in general) referred to me as "gay." This reading practice (of placing me on one end of a sexual-orientation binary) reflects what I will soon argue is a desire by many people to think of sexual orientation in ways that do not trouble their own sexual identities. To see me as (and to call me) "gay" is comforting because "gay" puts me on the "other" side of the binary. To see me as "bisexual" or "queer" is to acknowledge that sexual identity is not either-or but much more fluid, and that is not a concept that many were/ are willing to embrace. They were resisting, in other words, the discomforting departure from binaries (e.g., straight-gay, self-other).

2. In the essay, as in this chapter, I used the term *queer* to mean "gay, lesbian, bisexual, transgender, intersexed (neither male nor female) or in other ways

'queer' because of one's sexual identity or sexual orientation." In addition to its inclusiveness, I choose to use the term *queer* for its pedagogical effect and political significance. As I will later argue, the term *queer* is discomforting to many people because it continues to invoke a history of bigotry and hatred, but for many queers, it has come to signify a rejection of normative sexualities and genders, a reclaiming of the terms of their identities, and a feeling of self-empowerment (Tierney and Dilley, 1998).

3. It is true that heterosexism is brought up in the essay more often than other forms of oppression, but only slightly. I could not help but wonder if the reason students felt that heterosexism was given "too much emphasis" was because it was not given the kind of emphasis that it is normally given, by which I mean, only marginal attention. Perhaps my students could have tolerated a superficial discussion in which heterosexism was tokenized, but were unable and unwilling to mask their resistance to change when confronted with heterosexism head on.

REFERENCES

Britzman, D. P. (1998a). *Lost subjects, contested objects: Toward a psychoanalytic inquiry of learning*. Albany: State University of New York Press.

Britzman, D. P. (1998b). On some psychical consequences of AIDS education. In W. F. Pinar (Ed.), *Queer theory in education*. Mahweh, NJ: Lawrence Erlbaum.

Ellsworth, E. (1992). Why doesn't this feel empowering? Working through the repressive myths of critical pedagogy. In C. Luke & J. Gore (Eds.), *Feminisms and critical pedagogies*. New York: Routledge.

Ellsworth, E. (1997). *Teaching positions: Difference, pedagogy, and the power of address*. New York: Teachers College Press.

Felman, S. (1995). Education and crisis, or the vicissitudes of teaching. In C. Caruth (Ed.), *Trauma: Explorations in memory*. Baltimore, MD: Johns Hopkins University Press.

Freire, P. (1970). *Pedagogy of the oppressed*. (Translated by M. B. Ramos.) New York: Continuum.

Giroux, H. A., & McLaren, P. L. (1989). Introduction: Schooling, cultural politics, and the struggle for democracy. In H. A. Giroux & P. McLaren (Eds.), *Critical pedagogy, the state, and cultural struggle*. Albany: State University of New York Press.

Kumashiro, K. K. (1999). "Barbie," "big dicks," and "faggots": Paradox, performativity, and anti-oppressive pedagogy. *JCT: The Journal of Curriculum Theorizing, 15*(1), 27–42.

Kumashiro, K. K. (2000). Toward a theory of anti-oppressive education. *Review of Educational Research, 70*(1), 25–53.

Lather, P. (1998). Critical pedagogy and its complicities: A praxis of stuck places. *Educational Theory, 48*(4), 487–497.

Tierney, W. G., & Dilley, P. (1998). Constructing knowledge: Educational research and gay and lesbian studies. In W. F. Pinar (Ed.), *Queer theory in education*. Mahweh, NJ: Lawrence Erlbaum.

CHAPTER 11

Bridging Multicultural Education:
Bringing Sexual Orientation into the Children's and Young Adult Literature Classrooms

Patti Capel Swartz

> School was one of the more painful experiences of my youth.
> The neighborhood bullies could be avoided. The taunts of the
> children living in those endless repetitive row houses could be
> evaded by staying in my room. But school was something I had
> to face day after day for some two hundred mornings a year.
> —Tommi Avicolli, playwright and activist (1998)

As Avicolli (1998) notes, attending school is mandatory. There is, short of dropping out, no way of avoiding the pain that results from physical and psychological abuse: the taunts of schoolmates, the sense of isolation from others, and a lack of protection on the part of teachers or administrators. Because I have worked with lesbian, gay, bisexual, transgendered, or intersexed (hereafter l/g/b/t/i) students in universities in Georgia, Kentucky, and Ohio inside and out of the classroom, I am very aware that the pain of elementary and high school is often overwhelming and leaves scars that take years to heal, if they ever do. I am also aware that heterosexual students are often not aware of the depth of pain that their taunts or silence creates, for cultural messages tell them that hate speech toward l/g/b/t/i students is allowable. Because name-calling and ridicule begin in elementary school, I believe it is vital to begin interrogation of attitudes toward sexuality in elementary education. While the past 20 years have shown gains in including African American, Mexican, Latina/o, Chicana/o, Asian American, and Native American experience in curricula, the same is certainly not true for literature that includes experiences of l/g/b/t/i persons. Too few states or school districts attempt to defuse the prejudices that are apparent in schools and in the greater culture.

In her essay "Homophobia, Why Bring It Up?" African American activist and writer Barbara Smith notes: "Homophobia is usually the last oppression to be mentioned, the last to be taken seriously, the last to go. But it is extremely serious, sometimes to the point of being fatal" (1999, p. 112). Smith continues:

> Curriculum that focuses in a positive way upon issues of sexual identity, sexuality, and sexism is still rare . . . yet schools are virtual cauldrons of homophobic sentiment, as witness by everything from the graffiti in the bathrooms and the putdowns yelled on the playground to the heterosexist bias of most texts and the firing of teachers on no other basis than that they are not heterosexual. (p. 114)

As an African American lesbian, Smith understands that none of our lives are based on one single issue like sexuality, and that one way to understand the complexity and nature of intersecting and overlapping oppressions, and stereotypes, is to look at them in combination in the classroom:

> Making connections between oppressions is an excellent way to introduce the subjects of lesbian and gay male identity and homophobia, because it offers people a frame of reference on which to build. . . . It is factually inaccurate and strategically mistaken to present the materials as if all gay people were white and male. (p. 115)

At the regional campus in Appalachian Ohio where I teach it is vital for education majors who are mostly White working-class students, often first-generation college students, who have strong ties to fundamental religious beliefs, that issues that interrogate race, class, and gender, including l/g/b/t/i issues, be included in the curriculum. Certainly the violence of the past few years, frequent gay-bashing, the well-publicized death of Matthew Shepard, and shootings at numerous schools around the country (which are often related in some way to sexism or to sexual innuendo) indicate the need for students to examine and change the prejudices that are so widely held. Warren Blumenfeld (1993) points out that "issues relating to GLBT people should be formally and permanently integrated into existing courses across the curriculum" and "homophobia and other 'diversity' workshops should be implemented for the entire campus community to sensitize and educate staff, faculty, and administrators." Mary Elliot (1996) writes that by not including l/g/b/t/i issues in classroom discussion and materials, and not attempting to lessen homophobia, lesbian and gay teachers who remain in the closet "may find themselves in the position of protecting the very institutions that exclude them, and their students, from full participation" (p. 699) in the university community, in the classroom, and in the culture.

I believe that the most important classes in which to include multicultural issues are children's and young adult literature classes, for if future teachers are without awareness of the issues and of the literature that can counter racism, classism, ableism, sexism, and homophobia, attitudes and practices in schools will not change. When such intervention does not occur we face high drop-out rates for l/g/b/t/i teens; the highest teen suicide rate of any group; and hate crimes of teens who physically abuse or murder l/g/b/t/i people, or people who seem so to them, or the hate crimes of students who feel they have been targeted as objects of ridicule. The words of choice used to denigrate others from early elementary through high school include *gay, faggot, lezzie, dyke,* and *homo.* As teacher Cora Sangree says in Debra Chasoff and Helen S. Cohen's (1995) film *It's Elementary: Talking about Gay Issues in Schools,* "Kids hear this information all the time [and what they hear] reinforces stereotypes." Sangree notes that in discussing gay issues, she talks about gays with regard to community and culture, "not gay sex. Talking about gay sex is not appropriate."

L/g/b/t/i issues can be brought into the classroom in the same way as any other multicultural issues: through literature, discussion, and writing. Some states mandate antihomophobic education, but when states, school districts, and school boards do not, teachers may have to educate themselves. An excellent starting place is Chasoff and Cohen's film, a film I use in Children's Literature classes. *It's Elementary* provides both insights into prejudices and homophobia and methods for examining homophobia, stereotypes, and prejudices in the language arts or social studies classroom. In the film, Daithe Wolfe, a teacher in Madison, Wisconsin, notes that the standard curriculum already holds many ways to introduce gay history and gay issues. Both he and Robert Roth, a California social studies teacher, use webbing or mapping as ways of creating connections, examining stereotypes, and entering discussion. Webbing and mapping are both common brainstorming strategies in language arts (and other subject area) classrooms that help students prepare for writing. In full-class discussion, students provide terms and ideas related to a central theme such as homophobia. The instructor records these contributions on a chalkboard or whiteboard, connecting them to the central concept, which is placed in a circle at center, and to each other by means of diagrammatic lines. In this way, students gain access to others' perceptions of the concept, often clarify their own thinking, and develop ideas and gain assistance with organization for writing. Roth uses free writing as a follow-up to the mapping discussion.

As Chasoff and Cohen's film shows, literature is also used for discussion. Cambridge Friends School teachers use *Asha's Mums*, by Rosamund Elwin and Michelle Paulse (1990), and illustrated by Dawn Lee, with early elementary students as a way of providing insights, understanding, and empathy and as a way of developing a sense of justice. In this picture book, Asha's class is going on a field trip. Her teacher, however, won't accept Asha's permission slip because it is signed by both of her mothers. She tells Asha that she can't have two mothers. Student discussion shows that the students understand Asha's position, and how hurt and upset her teacher's actions make her, just how unjust these actions are.

While materials are fairly easy to integrate, without background knowledge about gender and sexuality, teachers may be reluctant to include materials about sexuality and gender because of fear of name-calling during discussion. However, in their essay "Locating a Place for Gay and Lesbian Themes in Elementary Reading, Writing, and Talking," James R. King and Jennifer Jasinski Schneider (1999) write that responses to name-calling can open up real discussion about "why such talk is harmful and inappropriate" (p. 126). Although King and Schneider's work focuses on early elementary school experience, discussing name-calling as "an intent to demean" (p. 127) through the use of the power of language has not lost its potency for discussion in the classroom, kindergarten through college, particularly because the names used, while common in school hallways, are seldom addressed. Such discussions reveal the underlying necessity of the negativity of terms that demean l/g/b/t/i people—and women—to heterosexual regulation of the population. Such discussions can illuminate how these are a part of the "mechanisms behind sexist, patriarchal notions of masculinity" (p. 128) that so often deprive women, whether heterosexual, lesbian, bisexual, or intersex or transgender, of the rights and opportunities to live full lives and to achieve all of which they are capable.

Chasoff and Cohen's film looks at these issues. It also dispels the stereotype that only l/g/b/t/i people feel that gay issues in school are important or that neutrality is desirable. In "Coming Out in the Classroom," Mary Elliot (1996) points out that despite what teachers would like to suppose, the classroom is not neutral, for "neutrality . . . is a universal cultural default setting which is almost always presumed to be heterosexual and white; it is not available to those who cannot 'pass' as either or both" (p. 698). As Elliot indicates, the gay teacher "coming out [in the classroom] challenges dominant thinking and institutional heterosexism [and] provides a model and personal contact for gay, lesbian, and heterosexual students alike, facilitating the unlearning of prejudice" (p. 698). This "challenge" to "dominant thinking" applies, however, whether or not the teacher is l/g/t/b/i or heterosexual, for the normativity and naturalization of heterosexuality must be challenged if all children are to benefit from education. As James Sears (1999) points out, challenging stereotypical ideas about gender and sexuality requires educators who "model honesty, civility, authenticity, integrity, fairness, and respect" while "creating classrooms that challenge categorical thinking, promote interpersonal intelligence, and foster critical consciousness" (pp. 4–5).

Wayne Martino (1999) writes that teachers can "help students interrogate familiar patterns of thinking that often resort to defining sexual identity in oppositional terms and as a stable category" (p. 137), allowing interrogation of "compulsory heterosexuality" and the binary oppositions of male/female and heterosexual/homosexual that have been enforced through patriarchy and compulsory heterosexuality. Martino analyzes student responses and experiences of six teachers in a Catholic high school that had as eighth-grade required reading Morris Gleitzman's (1993) novel *Two Weeks With the Queen*, the story of a boy who is sent away from home because his brother is dying. He becomes friends with a gay man whose partner is dying of AIDS. Although Martino notes that teachers "tended . . . to work with liberal humanist notions of identity . . . that allowed students to challenge particular stereotypes about gay men" (a strategy that primarily provokes tolerance), student responses indicated a high level of involvement with the text, which opens the possibility for teaching that will result in "interrupting heteronormativity" to move "beyond positions of mere acceptance and tolerance of the other to encourage students to think about what we take for granted as 'normal' and 'natural'" (pp. 135–139, 147). Because heterosexuality is socially constructed as "normal" in our culture, the wide range of sexualities possible for humans is largely ignored by many educators. Perceived gender roles are also closely related to sexuality in narrow definitions that privilege heterosexuality.

While investigation of sexual acts and sexual activity is not appropriate for children, investigation of gender roles and the ways that sexuality is characterized in those narrow cultural definitions is appropriate. Such investigation can start with such simple concepts as expected gender roles and social practices, showing how social constructions affect notions of sexuality. For instance, pink is for girls and blue for boys; girls play with dolls and boys with trucks; mothers and girls are "nurturing," while fathers and boys are "strong" and, in the case of fathers, "disciplinarians." Socially constructed expectations of families can also be investigated by the use of discussion, mapping and clustering, and writing that asks children to identify the makeup of families that they know about from their experience and from reading. As Martino (1999) notes, "There are tremendous possibilities for teachers to engage students in this kind of critical work" (p. 148). Such interrogation may be a part of critical looks at many either/or (binary) social constructions. As Suzanne Pharr (1998) points out, "It is virtually impossible to view one oppression . . . in isolation because they are all connected: sexism, racism, homophobia, classism, ableism, anti-Semitism, ageism" (p. 53). Pharr notes that oppressions are not possible without "common elements" that include a "defined norm" that is backed up by "institutional power, economic power, and both institutional and individual violence": "The combination of these three elements . . . makes complete control possible" (p. 53). Looking at families, friendships, and relationships critically with regard to the ways in which concepts are passed on through culture can continue on into the ways in which love, friendship, and concepts of family become limited in scope in cultures constructed to privilege binary oppositions. Students can begin to understand the ways in which narrow conceptions not only limit our humanity but also create stereotypes, prejudices, racism, sexism, and homophobia. Such critical thinking calls into question those mores that are so often taken for granted not only by children, but by adults as well.

Students can explore the ways categories created through the use of two oppositional pronouns such as *he* and *she*, or *hers* and *his* work. Who is included in those pronouns? Who is excluded? If a child who is narrowly defined as "male" is not interested in the gender roles "normally" associated with male children, how is that child treated? What terms are often used for ridicule? How do these terms reflect the values that this culture places on "male" and "female" identity? How do the constructions of gender and sexuality that they represent allow enfranchisement or disenfranchisement? How do sexism, heterosexism, and homophobia work together to constrain sexuality and gender and to punish transgression of these categories?

Sexual and gender constructions have become "naturalized" through the expectations that they create, yet critical examination shows the ways in which they fail. As Minnie Bruce Pratt (1998) writes of Leslie Feinberg, these dualistic pronouns cannot capture the complexity of his/her existence. Pratt realizes this inadequacy when the possibilities for sexual identification are reduced to the either/or of the masculine or feminine. Jess, Feinberg's character in her novel *Stone Butch Blues* realizes that whether she is a man or a woman "could never be answered as long as those were the only choices" (1993, p. 222). In *Gender Outlaw* Kate Bornstein (1994) writes of being a woman trapped in a man's body who underwent a sex change operation in order to feel "whole." Bornstein writes: "The choice between two of something is not a choice at all, but rather the opportunity to subscribe to the value system which holds the two presented choices as mutually exclusive alternatives" (p. 101). In much the same way that activist Suzanne Pharr notes that fear helps to control women and sexuality and that homophobia bolsters heterosexism, Bornstein notes that she once "tacitly support[ed] all the rules of the gender system . . . in order to belong, or rather to not be an outsider" (p. 101). She points out that defense of gender and sexual boundaries leads to gay bashing and the murder of gays and lesbians and that the violence of gay bashing has much to do with punishment for "violat[ing] the rules of gender in this culture" (p. 105). Like Pharr, Bornstein realizes, "The most obviously violent structure within the cult of gender is sexism, misogyny. Misogyny is necessary to maintain the cult of gender" (105).

Children can understand and need to understand that words can be effective weapons and that seemingly innocuous words, particularly sexist language that reflects constructions formed though employment of binary oppositions, can be used to hurt and to control. They need to be helped to look beyond prejudices to understand the ways in which particular sexist words that are used to denigrate l/g/b/t/i people and differently gendered people reflect cultural denigration of women as well. For instance, categories of male and female have words that are closely related to sexual and gender constructions. For example, because love of flowers is typically constructed as "female," the term *pansy* when applied to "males" implies an un-"masculine" softness, "female" identification, and denigration. *Sissy*, so often applied to men who appear to be gay, transgendered, or intersexed, comes from *sister*. If this term is a derogatory word when applied to "males," then it reflects the underlying misogyny in the culture. And *faggot*, the most common term of denigration in schools today, refers to the bundles of wood gathered to kindle the fires to burn witches during the Middle Ages in Europe, witches who were usually female.

Gender and sex bias in language used against l/g/b/t/i people is stronger and more hurtful when applied to "male" children than when applied to young girls. While derogatory, the term *tomboy*, when applied to a girl, does not have the stigma associated with *sissy*, *pansy*, or other terms commonly used to denigrate young gay men, or those who appear to be gay. Disputing prejudices, interrupting taken-for-granted assumptions, and helping children to unlearn the prejudices and often deadly biases transmitted through culture requires understanding of the ways in which binary oppositions in language are implicated in keeping homophobia, racism, sexism, classism, and other "isms" used to denigrate particular individuals or populations alive, and even very young children can engage in in-

terrogation of the constructions of language that reinforce binary oppositions of these sorts and homophobia.

Children can theorize about homophobia, sexuality, and gender roles
with knowledge that can be enhanced and enlarged through reading, and
attitudes can change. As Gloria Anzaldúa (1990) writes: "Theory produces
effects that change people and the way they perceive the world. Thus we
need teorías . . . that will rewrite history using race, class, gender and
ethnicity as categories of analysis" (pp. xxv–xxvi). Materials that are helpful
in such critical thinking, theorizing, and discussing include *Asha's Mums*,
which combats internalized oppression and forwards social justice as well
as creating understanding of varying constructions of family. Some other
valuable picture books include Barbara Lynn Edmonds's *Mama Eat Ant,
Yuck!* (2000), Joseph Kennedy's *Lucy Goes to the Country* (1998), Lesléa
Newman's *Heather Has Two Mommies* (1989), Johnny Valentine's *One Dad,
Two Dads, Brown Dad, Blue Dads* (1994), and Michael Willhoite's *Daddy's
Roommate* (1991). Books suitable for older children include Marion Dane
Bauer's *Am I Blue? Coming out of the Silence* (1994); several of Chris Crutcher's
(1991, 1995) sports/adventure novels; James Haskins's (1998) biography
of Bayard Rustin; Gigi Kaeser's *Love Makes a Family* (1999); and Jacqueline
Woodson's *From the Notebooks of Melanin Sun* (1995) and *The House You Pass
on the Way* (1999); both of which take on stereotypical constructions of
race, gender, and sexuality. Kevin Jennings's *Becoming Visible: A Reader in
Gay and Lesbian History for High School and College Students* (1994) is appropriate for middle school as well as high school children.

I have found it helpful to be very open and honest with students,
discussing my own internalized prejudices and how I continually work
toward awareness and lessening of these. Incorporating interrogation of
heterosexuality, discussing a continuum of sexuality and the diversity of
choices of gender roles as in Tomie dePaola's *Oliver Button Is a Sissy* (1979)
allows sex and gender to be seen in ways that are neither stereotypical
nor prejudicial. It is possible to go beyond the usual depiction of homo-
sexuality as being only about sexuality without regard for the complexity
of a whole person, and to point out as Cora Sangree does in *It's Elementary*, that l/g/b/t/i people form communities, hold jobs, go to school, live
in families, create families, and build friendships. In that film, Noé Gutierrez
makes an additional point often overlooked when school administrators,
teachers, and community members have conversations about gay materials and issues in schools. He notes that the idea is often that "gay people
are coming to our schools"—as though no gay children are present in
schools. But, Gutierrez notes, "I was a [gay] child, and I was in school."
He continues, pointing out that neither speakers nor materials that combat homophobia are bringing "something or someone" to the classroom

that is not already there. In *It's Elementary* teacher Thelma Delgado-Josey tells of homophobia that was endemic in the Puerto Rican culture of which she was a part. She had to overcome the homophobia she had learned, but she has done this, for because of the racism and invisibility that was directed toward her and her culture, she knows what it is like "not to be affirmed in the classroom because I was not as a child." From her experience, Delgado-Josey realizes that "being there" for her students includes creating a safe space for difference, whether that difference involves race, gender, sexuality, class, or ability.

As teachers, we need to deconstruct the biases of education to allow all our students to think critically and to live full and vital lives. As philosopher/educator Glorianne Leck (1999) writes: "It is unacceptable to deprive children of credible information about their sexuality, about human and social diversity, and about the abuse of power within families, within schools, and within religious group relationships." We can, as Leck notes, move "forward into new opportunities for dialogue that can dramatically, dynamically, and subtly open vital new possibilities for more reflective and just practices of schooling" (260).

REFERENCES

Anzaldúa, G. (1990). Haciendo caras, una entrada. In G. Anzaldúa (Ed.), *Making face, making soul = Haciendo caras: Creative and critical perspectives by feminists of color* (pp. xv–xxvii). San Francisco: Aunt Lute Foundation Books.

Avicolli, T. (1998). He defies you still: The memoirs of a sissy. In P. S. Rothenberg (Ed.), *Race, class and gender in the United States: An integrated study* (4th ed., pp. 328–333). New York: St. Martins.

Bauer, Marion Dane (Ed.). (1994). *Am I blue? Coming out from the silence.* New York: HarperCollins.

Blumenfeld, W. J. (1993). *Making Colleges and Universities Safe for Gay, Lesbian, Bisexual, and Transgender Students and Staff: Report and Recommendations of the Massachusettes Governor's Commission on Gay and Lesbian Youth.* Retrieved March 8, 2008, from http://www.lbgtcampus.org/resources/making_college_safe.html

Bornstein, K. (1994). *Gender outlaw: On men, women, and the rest of us.* New York: Vintage.

Chasoff, D., & Cohen, H. S. (1995). *It's elementary: Talking about gay essues in school.* Harriman, NY: New Day Films.

Crutcher, C. (1991). *Athletic shorts.* New York: William Morrow.

Crutcher, C. (1995). *Ironman.* New York: Laurel-Leaf.

dePaola, T. (1979). *Oliver Button is a sissy.* San Diego, CA: Harcourt Brace.

Edmonds, B. L. (2000). *Mama eat ant, yuck!* Eugene, OR: Hundredth Munchy.

Elliot, M. (1996). "Coming Out in the Classroom." *College English, 58,* 693–708.

Elwin, R., & Paulse, M. (1990). *Asha's mums* (Dawn Lee, Illus.). Toronto, Ontario, Canada: Women's Press.

Feinberg, L. (1993). *Stone butch blues: A novel.* Ithaca: Firebrand.

Gleitzman, M. (1993). *Two weeks with the queen.* New York: HarperCollins.

Haskins, J. (1998). *Bayard Rustin: Behind the scenes of the civil rights movement.* New York: Hyperion.

Jennings, K. (Ed.). (1994). *Becoming visible: A reader in gay and lesbian history for high school and college students.* Los Angeles: Alyson.

Kaeser, G. (1999). *Love makes a family.* Cambridge, MA: University of Massachusetts Press.

Kennedy, J. (1998). *Lucy goes to the country.* Los Angeles: Alyson.

King, J. R., & Schneider, J. J. (1999). Locating a place for gay and lesbian themes in elementary reading, writing, and talking. In W. J. Letts & J. T. Sears (Eds.), *Curriculum, cultures, and (homo) sexualities: vol. 1. Queering elementary education: Advancing the dialogue about sexualities and schooling* (pp. 125–136). Lanham, MD: Rowman and Littlefield.

Leck, G. M. (1999). Afterword. In W. J. Letts & J. T. Sears (Eds.), *Curriculum, cultures, and (homo) sexualities: vol. 1. Queering elementary education: Advancing the dialogue about sexualities and schooling* (pp. 257–262). Lanham, MD: Rowman and Littlefield.

Martino, W. (1999). "It's okay to be gay": Interrupting straight thinking in the English classroom. In W. J. Letts & J. T. Sears (Eds.), *Curriculum, cultures, and (homo) sexualities: vol. 1. Queering elementary education: Advancing the dialogue about sexualities and schooling* (pp. 137–149). Lanham, MD: Rowman and Littlefield.

Newman, L. (1989). *Heather has two mommies.* Los Angeles: Alyson.

Pharr, S. (1998). *Homophobia: A weapon of sexism.* Little Rock, AR: Chardon Press.

Pratt, M. B. (1996). *S/HE.* Ithaca, NY: Firebrand.

Sears, J. T. (1999). Teaching Queerly: Some Elementary Propositions. In W. J. Letts & J. T. Sears (Eds.), *Curriculum, cultures, and (homo) sexualities: vol. 1. Queering elementary education: Advancing the dialogue about sexualities and schooling* (pp. 3–14). Lanham, MD: Rowman and Littlefield.

Smith, B. (1999). Homophobia: Why bring it up? *The truth that never hurts: Writings on race, gender, and freedom* (pp. 111–115). New Brunswick, NJ: Rutgers University Press.

Valentine, J. (1994). *One dad, two dads, brown dad, blue dads.* Los Angeles, CA: Alyson.

Willhoite, M. (1991). *Daddy's roommate.* Los Angeles, CA: Alyson.

Woodson, J. (1995). *From the notebooks of Melanin Sun.* New York: Scholastic.

Woodson, J. (1999). *The house you pass on the way.* New York: Laurel-Leaf.

CHAPTER 12

Nuns, Midwives, and Witches: Women's Studies in the Elementary Classroom

Sarah Napier

IN MAY 1989, during Columbia University's graduation ceremony, a 140-foot-long banner bearing the names of Charlotte Brontë, Emily Dickinson, and Virginia Woolf was unfurled over the facade of the university library. Over the columned, imposing gray stone of the library—inscribed with the names of Plato, Cicero, Virgil—the banner flapped in the wind. It was impermanent, but carrying a clear message: Women's achievements merit them a place among the "great scholars."

This message is inscribing itself into our consciousness. College courses have become notably more progressive in recent years, even though most of what is taught at the high school and elementary level remains more traditional. As a 1st-year teacher of 10- and 11-year-olds, at Paideia School in Atlanta, Georgia, I was determined to take what I had learned in college into my classroom. I was determined not to stereotype the girls and boys in my class according to traditional sex roles, and I wanted the subjects I taught to be inclusive of women. Encouraging equality between girls and boys and promoting assertive behavior in girls should be complemented and given strength in a classroom's subject matter. Girls and young women receive many mixed messages—from families, friends, and especially the media. The message they deserve from teachers should be clear and consistent: Your sex deserves equal treatment, and that includes giving women a place and a voice in the material we study.

Paideia School is a private open-classroom school, founded in 1971. The school community is committed to progressive education. What has emerged from this commitment is a school of 600 students, with classes beginning at the preschool level and continuing through high school. Elementary classes are mixed aged and nongraded, with 30 children and two teachers in every classroom. Paideia offers the individual teacher freedom and support. Curriculum content is discussed at faculty meetings, but within some basic guidelines there is encouragement of creativity and innovation. The school works to treat each child individually and to value the autonomy of each teacher. The student population is fairly diverse, and 10% of the students receive financial aid.

Peter Richards, with whom I teach, has concentrated on the Middle Ages as a central subject in his classroom for several years. We teach the history of the period, focusing on daily life; our students do art projects such as stained glass, calligraphy, or Celtic design; we perform a medieval solstice play; we read fictional stories about medieval life. Peter's approach to the Middle Ages challenges the students to imagine themselves in medieval times: What was life like for 11-year-olds in the Middle Ages? This treatment of the Middle Ages gave me the opportunity to integrate more focus on women into Peter's existing curriculum. I wanted girls to see themselves and their ancestors as part of the history we explore. If the only reference points a girl has are monks, kings, and Viking warriors, it is unlikely that she will feel a connection to the time period. I also wanted boys to see beyond any preconceived ideas about the Middle Ages to acknowledge women's contributions and experiences.

Since the majority of medieval women could not read or write, they left few accounts of their lives. What medieval men wrote about women was either a romanticized version of the "fair lady in distress" or a condemnation of women based on the sin of Eve. Several recent books, however, offer a more accurate representation of women's lives (see the "Course Materials" section).

When studied with a feminist approach, the lives of women in the Middle Ages are fascinating. Medieval women were painfully oppressed by the patriarchal Catholic Church, and they were physically vulnerable to the dangers of bearing children in a time of primitive medical care. Medieval women were also powerful and competent, managing large households while men were away at war. It is exciting to explore what traditional sources had to say about women and how later historians use primary sources such as manor records to piece together more accurate information about women's lives. The challenge is to make the material accessible to children, while respecting the harsh realities of life for most medieval women.

There are some inherent problems with teaching 10- and 11-year-olds about the Middle Ages in a nonsexist way. Boys are drawn to the pageantry of knights, castles, and war. Within the 1st week of school this year, four boys had brought in books about the Middle Ages from home and asked to borrow books from the class. A group of boys were also building models of knights. I struggled with the dilemma of how to excite girls about the topic without overwhelming them with the stark and grim quality of life for medieval women. Traditional activities such as cooking or sewing seemed a poor contrast to the pageantry of conflict.

Peter usually started the year off with the discussion of childbirth, and I was able to expand what he had already covered to include more extensive discussion of midwives and other women healers. We asked the kids to share stories from their own births, and then together we asked questions. What might be different about having a baby in the Middle Ages? Were there doctors in the Middle Ages? How many children did women usually have? Did all of them usually live? Did people understand that sex led to pregnancy? To end the discussion, children, boys and girls both, closed their eyes and tried to imagine themselves as a woman in the Middle Ages who had just discovered she was pregnant. How did they feel? Were they scared? Elated? Angry? What were their chances of survival? Most described themselves as afraid. We ended on a sobering note, concluding that fear of dying in childbirth was probably the biggest issue in most medieval women's lives.

Our first discussion set the tone for the rest of the year. We had launched our study with something accessible and real to our students. Every student had a story to tell about his or her own birth, and the class was intrigued by all the superstitions and seemingly strange practices surrounding birth in the Middle Ages. I think it is valuable to have boys imagine themselves in a situation like pregnancy that is uniquely female. This begins to give them some perspective on the female experience, an understanding that will become increasingly important in their relationships with girls and women.

During the year, we studied a variety of topics relating to peasant women, queens, marriage, and witchcraft. As part of our study of the Catholic Church, we studied monasteries and convents. The class was more receptive to any topic if Peter or I could tell them a good story about it. But because there is so little known about individual women's lives, finding such stories is a challenge. The life of Hildegarde of Bingen, an abbess during the 11th century, lent itself to colorful storytelling.

At the end of our Catholicism study, Peter asked a Grey nun to talk to the class about her decision to become a nun and about her spiritual life. She spoke openly about her loneliness when she joined the convent at the age of 16 and of her family's begging her to return home. It was important for this study to conclude with a visit from a modern woman whose life had some similarities to that of the medieval women we had studied.

Another way to encourage students' curiosity is to let them learn about something while experiencing it with all of their senses. We could explore the more traditional female roles while cooking a medieval dish or planting herbs. We hired an accomplished weaver, Paula Vester, to come into our classroom and talk to the kids about spinning and weaving in the Middle Ages and to teach the students to use a drop spindle—a simple spinning device common in medieval times and still used in some parts of the world today. Once the children became accomplished spinners, we spun and dyed (using Vidalia onion skins) enough wool on one of the weaver's looms to make a small table runner. Both girls and boys were excited enough to stay in at lunch to spin and weave.

Our study of the Middle Ages concluded as each student did an individual project, which was to include a written report and some sort of three-dimensional component such as a model or a costume. I was hopeful that some students, without too much prodding, would pick topics relating to women. The students who chose topics relating to women did an excellent job and showed sensitivity toward the complexity of medieval women's lives. A student who studied witchcraft found a modern version of a Wiccan ritual dating from medieval times, which she performed for her report.

One student reached these conclusions about Eleanor of Aquitaine: "She gained respect for women by using her power as a queen. . . . She established women's rights. . . . She was the first woman to want and get a divorce." Another student wrote the following about her topic, medieval midwives:

> The church disliked women and anything that had to do with healing. The reason the church disliked women is because of the sin of Eve. The reason the church disliked healing is because they thought if you were sick then God meant for you to be, and healers should not interfere with God's wishes. Also the fact that midwives were associated with witchcraft disturbed the church as well.

There were not as many reports about women as I would have liked, but since the whole class listened to all of the reports, students were at least exposed to several topics relating to women. One thing I'd like to work on this year is finding more books about medieval women that are accurate and accessible to young students.

Unfortunately, none of the boys in the class picked topics concerning women. One of my goals for this year is to encourage boys to study a broader range of topics. And I want to challenge girls to pick the topics they tend to shy away from because they are stereotyped as "boys' stuff," such as the Battle of Hastings or Viking ships. The boys had an easier time picking topics for their reports than the girls did. It was obvious that the girls were not just being less assertive; our presentation of the topic was still geared more toward male interests. There were also reactions that disappointed me, such as that of the student who wrote in his journal at the end of the year: "I understand why we study the Vikings, but I still don't understand why it was important to study childbirth." The Middle Ages was a difficult time to be a woman or a young girl; women were regarded as evil and manipulative, or as delicate creatures in need of protection. While I may find studying about the hardships of women's lives fascinating, it is a heavy topic for a 10-year-old.

Girls often had clear, emotional responses to the material I presented on women in the Middle Ages. This made it easy to chose topics of study and to measure what kind of impact it was having on the girls I teach. It was more difficult for me to gauge the boys' reaction to their exposure to women's studies. As the year went on, I thought about strategies to help boys overcome their reluctance to study female issues. Since 11-year-old girls love any opportunity to gang up on "the boys," I tried to keep the focus specific to the Middle Ages. I let my students come up with generalizations and opinions and tried not to judge them. Although I think it is important to use words such as *feminism, sexism,* and *oppression,* and to explain what these words mean to me, I also resorted to more neutral terminology when I felt boys were feeling victimized or anxious; I talked of *fair* versus *not fair,* or *powerful* versus *not powerful.*

At times lessons about medieval society led to discussions of 20th-century life. A talk about stereotyped images of women in art once led us to examine stereotypes of women and men in contemporary advertising. It was positive for the boys to share ways their sex was stereotyped in the Madison Avenue world of the "Marlboro Man." I relied on my intuition to tell me when it was time to push the boys to listen to something that might be uncomfortable, such as a discussion about witchcraft and the treatment of women suspected of being witches, and when it was time to change the subject entirely or to take a break. As I taught, it was helpful to listen to Peter's reactions and feelings as a male in the classroom. I think it was good for our students to see me teaching him, my co-worker, some new information about the Middle Ages. I knew I was making progress when for Christmas I received a card from one of my male students, with a hand-drawn picture of a jolly woman in a Santa Claus suit. Scrawled in huge letters across the top was the message "Ms. Claus wishes you a Merry Christmas!"

As I begin my 2nd year of teaching, I am more aware of the relationship between the content that I teach and the social issues facing my students. It is imperative for teachers to encourage equitable relationships between boys and girls and to challenge girls to take risks, to express their opinions assertively, and to feel free to be excited about learning. I want our classroom to be a place where girls and boys are not burdened with our culture's stereotypes about being male or female. Subtle things about a classroom can exclude women and girls. Every table in our classroom has a name relating to the Middle Ages; kids have assigned seats at a table for about 6 weeks. Last year our tables had names like Vikings, Knights, Anglo-Saxons, and Normans. This year our table names include Nuns, Midwives, Spinners, and Weavers. Visual representation of medieval women in various roles also conveys a message of equality.

Jane Austen (1817/1969) summed up the problem many of us have in learning history: "Real solemn history, I cannot be interested in. . . . The quarrels of popes and kings, with wars or pestilences in every page; the men all so good for nothing and hardly any women at all" (p. 108). Women's studies has a place in the elementary classroom. To teach girls about women of achievement who preceded them empowers them and provides them with role models. It is also important for boys to learn about women and to have female role models.

Teaching kids about the oppression of women may inspire them to work against it and to understand that sexism is related to the oppression of people of color and other groups. It is crucial for young girls to realize that some of the freedoms that they enjoy are the result of work and commitment from generations of women, and that there is still more work to be done. If students are taught a subject in a way that includes the female experience, one hopes they will be critical learners in future classes, and that they will be aware of a noninclusive curriculum when they see it. Finally, teaching history to include women's lives and experiences affords students a richer, more accurate understanding of the past. History is not just about the transfer of power; it is about human lives filled with the extraordinary and the mundane. The wonders of childbirth and baking bread and the terror of the Black Plague are as much a part of history as the Crusades or the Battle of Hastings.

Yesterday a student handed me a book she was reading called *Rome and the Romans*. "Sarah," she said, "Why aren't there any pictures of girls in this book?"

"Good question," I answered. "What do you think?"

REFERENCE

Austen, J. (1969). *Northanger Abbey*. In R. W. Chapman (Ed.), *The novels of Jane Austen* (3rd ed., Vol. 5). Oxford, England: Oxford University Press. (Original work published 1817).

COURSE MATERIALS

Adams, C. (1983). *From workshop to warfare*. Cambridge, England: Cambridge University Press.
> A clearly written and informative book about medieval women written for older elementary students.

Bourdillon, H. (1988). *Women as healers*. Cambridge, England: Cambridge University Press.
> An overview of women healers throughout history written for older elementary students.

Gies, F., & Gies, J. (1978). *Women in the Middle Ages*. New York: Crowell.
> An accessible book for adults that focuses on everyday life in the medieval world.

Konigsburg, E. L. (1973). *A proud taste for Scarlet and Miniver*. New York: Atheneum.
> A novel for older elementary students based on the life of Eleanor of Aquitaine.

Labarge, M. W. (1986). *A small sound of the trumpet*. Boston: Beacon Press.
> This was the first book I used. Written for adults, it provides interesting historical information from a feminist perspective.

Willard, C. C. (1984). *Christine de Pizan: Her life and works*. New York: Persea Books.
> Detailed historical and literary analysis for adults about a fascinating and gifted woman writer.

I have also found the publications on medieval women from the Society for Creative Anachronism helpful. They include a bimonthly journal on topics relating to the Middle Ages; they cover some detailed and unusual subjects, such as medieval cosmetics; and they always include recipes, instructions for making costumes, and other information helpful to teachers. The address is: Society for Creative Anachronism, Office of the Registry, P.O. Box 360743, Milpitas, CA 95035-0743.

PART V

Threats to Public Education: Testing, Tracking, and Privatization

CHAPTER 13

Leaving Public Education Behind

Stan Karp

It is a measure of how far the right is reaching that the left today finds itself defending the very existence of public education from the forces of privatization, commercialization, and even federal policy. Just 4 years after Republican presidential candidate Bob Dole campaigned on a platform of abolishing the Department of Education, the Bush administration came into office with a massive expansion of the federal role in education as its number one domestic priority. This time, however, the goal has not been to extend the federal government's historic role as a promoter of educational access and equity, but to replace it with a conservative agenda of punitive high-stakes testing, privatization, and market "reforms."

Bush's signature domestic policy initiative, the No Child Left Behind Act, currently has schools reeling as its impact unfolds in frightening detail. As many as 80% of the nation's public schools may find themselves labeled as schools "needing improvement," on the narrow basis of annual test scores and unreachable performance targets. Thanks to 2 decades of governors' education summits and the persistent urging of the Clinton administration, virtually all states have adopted new curriculum standards. These standards are of widely varying educational quality and relevance to what takes place in real schools. But NCLB puts states, districts, and schools under federal mandate to enforce the standards above all other considerations through annual state testing or else face losing federal funds. The scheme uses achievement gaps to label schools as "failures," without providing the resources or support needed to eliminate these gaps and includes an unfunded mandate that, by 2014, 100% of all students, including special education students and English-language learners, must be proficient on state tests. Schools that don't reach increasingly unattainable test score targets face an escalating series of sanctions up to and including possible closure and the imposition of private management on public schools.

Instead of an appropriate educational strategy, NCLB is part of a calculated political campaign to leave schools and children behind as the federal government retreats from the nation's historic commitment to improving universal public schooling for all children. The sanctions will do little to address the pressing needs of public schools but they will create a widespread perception of systemic failure, demoralize education workers, and erode the common ground that a universal system of public education needs to survive. The Bush scheme—passed, it should be noted, with overwhelming Democratic support—attempts to channel students and funds toward for-profit education management companies and revive an ideologically driven voucher movement that has been overwhelmingly defeated in every public referendum held so far. The Supreme Court's June 2002 decision endorsing the transfer of state and federal dollars to private and religious schools will accelerate this rightward turn in federal education policy, which includes assaults on long-standing and relatively successful social programs like Title I and Head Start. Using schools to promote military recruitment, school prayer, and even homophobia (a special provision guarantees the Boy Scouts access to school facilities despite its history of antigay discrimination) are all part of the toxic NCLB mix.

NCLB's obsessive overreliance on standardized tests in the name of accountability is more than bad education policy. It is a political effort to push other, more democratic approaches to school improvement aside. Currently, standardized curricula imposed through ever more suffocating layers of standardized testing constitute the primary agenda of antidemocratic schooling. When schools become obsessed with test scores, they narrow the focus of what teachers do in classrooms and limit teachers' ability to serve the broader needs of children and their communities. Overreliance on testing diverts attention and resources from more promising school improvement strategies like smaller schools and class size, multicultural curriculum reform, and collaborative professional development. High-stakes tests push struggling students out of school, promote tracking, and encourage schools to adopt developmentally inappropriate practices for younger children in an effort to "get them ready for the tests." Overuse of testing can also encourage cheating scandals and makes schools and students vulnerable to inaccurate and, at times, corrupt practices by commercial testing firms.

If the goal is educational accountability, standardized tests are of limited value. Assessing the effectiveness of a particular school or education program requires multiple measures of academic performance, including classroom observations and dialogue with real teachers and students, as well as a range of indicators from attendance and drop-out rates to graduation rates and postgraduation success, measures of teacher preparation and quality, surveys of parent participation and satisfaction, and similar evaluations. Legitimate assessment strategies would also measure "opportunity to learn" inputs and equity of resources so that the victims of educational failure were not the only ones to face "high stakes" consequences.

However, if the goal is a political one—to posture about "getting tough"; to drive multicultural curriculum reforms, equity concerns, and more pluralistic, bottom-up approaches to school reform out of the system; or to create a widespread general perception of school failure that can be used to justify "breaking up the public school monopoly"—then overreliance on standardized testing may do just fine.

Moreover, while inequality in test scores is one indicator of school performance, test scores also reflect other inequalities that persist in the larger society and in schools themselves. About 12% of White children live in poverty, while more than 30% of Black and Latino children live in poverty. The richest 1% of households has more wealth than the bottom 95%. Students in low-income schools, on average, have thousands of dollars less spent on their education than those in wealthier schools. About 14% of Whites don't have health insurance, but more than 20% of Blacks and 30% of Latinos have no health insurance. Unemployment rates for Blacks and Latinos are nearly double what they are for Whites.

Yet we do not hear the administration demanding an end to this kind of inequality. Nor do we hear the federal government saying all crime must be eliminated in 12 years or we'll privatize the police, all citizens must be healthy in 12 years or we will shut down the health care system.

Like all effective political strategies, the conservative school agenda speaks to real concerns held by large numbers of people, including concerns over low student achievement, the lack of institutional accountability, and the seemingly intractable school failure in low-income communities. These very real problems provide a platform for school reformers of all shapes and sizes to posture as champions of the underserved and underprivileged.

Bush, in particular, has made a career of such posturing. His trademark "compassionate conservatism" has always featured rhetorical attacks on the "soft bigotry of low expectations" and purports to focus attention on the real crisis of school failure in many poor communities. As a dubiously elected president who came into office with historically low levels of support among African Americans and a well-deserved antipoor, probusiness image, Bush uses education as an "outreach" issue. It's one of the few areas that allow a Republican president to posture, however disingenuously, as an ally of poor communities of color, particularly those that have been badly served by public education.

By focusing on the lowest-performing schools and the racial dimensions of the achievement gap, Bush gives his education rhetoric an edge and an urgency it would otherwise lack. However, he uses this rhetoric to frame policy proposals that actually reinforce the "hard bigotry" of institutional racism in education, for example, by promoting higher drop-out rates and perpetuating funding inequities. In fact, combining rhetorical concern for the victims of inequality with policies that perpetuate it may be an operative definition of "compassionate conservatism."

One key part of this effort involves a special appeal to parents, particularly in poor communities. In their voucher campaigns, conservatives have learned how to repackage market "reforms" that privatize public services as a form of "parental choice." Similarly, NCLB gives parents the right to take students and money out of struggling schools and to leave those schools behind. But it does not guarantee them any new places to go. In districts where some schools are labeled "failing" and some are not, the new law may actually force increased class sizes by transferring students without creating new capacity. NCLB does not invest in building new schools in failing districts. It does not make rich districts open their doors to students from poor districts. And it doesn't give poor parents any more control over school bureaucracies than food stamps give them over the supermarkets. The transfer regulations are a "supply side" formula designed to manufacture a demand for alternative school placements and ultimately to transfer funds and students to profit-making private school corporations through vouchers.

Such use of education standards and testing in the service of larger policy objectives is exactly what a number of Republican strategists have been proposing for years. As Nina Shokraii Rees (2001), a former Heritage Foundation researcher and advisor to Vice President Dick Cheney, wrote, "Standards, choice, and fiscal and legal autonomy in exchange for boosting student test scores increasingly are the watch-words of education reform in America. The principle can be used in programs that apply to whole districts as well as entire states. Importantly, it lays the groundwork for a massive overhaul of education at the federal level in much the same way that welfare reform began" (pp. 4–5).

NCLB is the culmination of a very active conservative mobilization around schools over the past several decades. It is also part of a larger political agenda that seeks to erode and privatize the public sector. The federal government provides only about 8% of school funding, but today the administration is using federal regulation to drive school policy in conservative directions at the state, district, and school levels. What's changed is not a new federal commitment to "leave no child behind," but the ideological commitment of some politicians to reform public education out of existence through a strategy of "test and burn." As researcher

Gerald Bracey (2003) has put it, NCLB "is a weapon of mass destruction and its target is the public schools."

The fallout from NCLB is beginning to generate a building resistance. In some places, students and parents are actively boycotting the imposition of high-stakes testing. Both major teacher unions, the National Education Association (NEA) and the American Federation of Teachers (AFT), are looking for ways to modify the worst NCLB provisions. Advocacy groups like Rethinking Schools, FairTest, and the Assessment Reform Network are trying to promote alternative accountability systems and approaches to reform that engage educators and communities in collaborative school improvement. Parent-community advocacy groups like the Association of Community Organizations for Reform Now (ACORN) are pressing politicians to make good on NCLB's rhetorical promises of better educational services for poor communities without gutting or privatizing the public system.

Together these efforts prefigure a movement that could project a vision of a democratic school reform that truly serves both children and society as a whole and that works to transform public education instead of destroying it. With NCLB making its noxious presence felt in a school district near you, it's a good time to find this resistance and join it.

REFERENCES

Bracey, G. (2003). April foolishness: The 20th anniversary of *A Nation at Risk*. *Phi Delta Kappan, 84*(8), 616–621. Retrieved March 8, 2008, from http://www .pdkintl.org/kappan/k0304bra.htm

Rees, N. (2001). *Improving education for every American child*. Washington, DC: Heritage Foundation.

CHAPTER 14

"I Plan to Be Somebody": The Absence of Tracking Is a Deeply Radical Idea

Nancy Barnes

> What I want out of my education is the sense that I will be se-
> cure in the future. That people won't look down at me because
> of where I come from. I don't want to be restricted to just one
> job. I want to have a choice. In this world an education is con-
> sidered important. You are most likely considered a nobody if
> you don't get an education. I plan to be somebody.
> —A high school junior, contemplating her future

IN HIS REMARKABLE book *Lives on the Boundary*, Mike Rose (1989) frames a haunting question that he has come to in his work with the diverse student populations scrambling to find their places in the university: "The basic question our society must ask, then, is: How many or how few do we want to have this education?" (p. 194).

For college teachers, especially those of us who are politically progressive people, crossing and recrossing the boundaries between intellectual work and activist projects, it's easy enough to say we want lots of young people, who represent many parts of American society, to have a liberal arts education. Or, as the young woman quoted above says, to have a choice. Our reasons for wanting this are myriad: the need for credentials in the labor market, the desire to see young people find meaningful work, or a vision of the changes that far-reaching diversity would bring to the institutions where we work. It's a great deal more difficult, however, to figure out how this can happen and what it demands of us.

The changing demographics of the United States are pressing racial, ethnic, and linguistic diversity on all institutions of higher education, whether they are ready or not. At the same time, the educational-opportunity programs and diversity initiatives that have supported these changes are under fierce political attack. Surprisingly, many college teachers seem to be unaware of how closely our fates are linked with those of the kids now graduating from high school and contemplating their future educations.

I have come to believe that college teachers must take responsibility for helping the young woman who says, "I plan to be somebody." Specifically, those of us at small private liberal arts colleges that pride themselves on their commitment to teaching must learn how to teach classes that represent a much broader spectrum than we are accustomed to encountering in our classrooms. My conviction has grown out of teaching in a collaborative project between Lang College, where I'm on the faculty, and several innovative high schools, leaders of school reform in New York City. The school I focus on here is Central Park East Secondary School, known as CPESS, a neighborhood high school in East Harlem.

CPESS designed the final 2 years of the secondary school to include "college courses," which would be taught by faculty members (like me) at college campuses in the New York City area. These courses were emphatically not designed for accelerated or academically "gifted" students; everyone at CPESS takes at least two such classes before graduation. The idea was to allow the kids to become familiar with university customs and requirements and to consider choices such as large versus small, public versus private, or racially diverse versus predominantly White campuses. Most important, the courses would invite the students, many of whom represent the first generation of their families to be educated beyond high school, to picture themselves as undergraduates at 4-year liberal arts institutions, to imagine having that life. The result, as I now know in my bones, is a far more complicated and genuine "mix" in every classroom than most academics can conceive of.

> The education I would need is first finish college, most likely I'll be going to John Jay Criminal Law School. Take LSAT into law school. Then I would go to law school. Get my Batchelors degree, I don't know in what, but then my master degree. It makes me feel like a person at the top of the list. A professional who has work hard in life to reach to the top of the ladder. Very proud of myself. (a high school senior, explaining her educational goals)

Teaching academically talented teenagers who are lost or angry or trapped by big city high schools was not new to me. I became a teacher somewhat serendipitously, by getting a job in a freshman-year program designed for kids desperate to get out of high school early. But this was different. As I got to know them, I realized that some of the students at

CPESS could easily have joined a freshman class on the spot. Others seemed unable to write a full paragraph, much less leave high school early.

Not only does CPESS intend to educate all of these young people, but the school rejects any "ability" groupings based on standardized tests or any other measure. Consequently, the students' choices are not governed by the systems of tracking and sorting that define American high schools. All of the Central Park East Secondary School students showed up in my "college" class together.

Mike Rose describes many of the students who are arriving on our campuses in increasing numbers as "underprepared." The language is useful, a beam of light that has helped me see as I've grappled with learning to teach untracked classes of high school students, some of whom are indeed underprepared.

This experience has stretched and altered the ways I have conceived of my own Freirian and feminist teaching practice. In capsule form, I've realized I have to help students learn the rules of what Lisa Delpit (1995) calls the university's "culture of power"; I have to pay extremely close attention to what it means to be a White teacher of students of color; and I have to be prepared to teach the skills that admit people into the academic club. Nothing has been as important, however, or as devastating, as realizing that I have to confront a fundamental privilege of college teaching, which is that I have literally never been expected to work with an untracked group of students.

> By now, I've taught many, many courses that explore how school operates as a mediating institution in state societies such as our own. Tracking is always a major part of the story. I often ask students to dredge up generative memories, in the Freirian sense of generative; one of my own is of my nephew Myles. Myles, a serious, redheaded 6-year-old, started school in a White, upper-middle-class suburb of Boston, a fancy town noted for its school system. When I asked him, early that fall, what his class was doing, he explained to me (I was in high school at the time) that you did different things depending on your group. "What groups?" I asked innocently. "Oh," said Myles, "the lions are the smart kids, the tigers are OK, and the giraffes are the kids who can't read or anything." (a college teacher (me), thinking about her first awareness of tracking)

The absence of tracking is a deeply radical idea, and it produces classrooms that are extremely demanding to teach. My course for the CPESS students was called Education in American Culture; it investigated how various perspectives in the social sciences might advance the students' thinking about this critical aspect of their lives. My idea for the course was OK, but I knew almost immediately that I was in a new world with these kids, that I scarcely knew how to hear their voices.

Listen to these fragments of student writing that suggest what it was like to encounter a totally untracked student group, really for the first time ever. I knew that wanting to "hear" their voices meant I had to give assignments in which the students could write about what they knew; they began to produce educational autobiographies, which then extended into the future. One African American boy wrote this (his text is uncorrected, as are all the student writings quoted here):

> I woke up this morning thinking of how hectic the day is going to be. I had to decide what suit I was going to where. About 7:30 am my wife had breakfast ready. I had to use my wife's car because my BMW M3 was in the shop. . . . [He continues, hour by hour through his morning.] At lunch I had a date with the Helmslys to talk of gaining a position of giving them a personal account and to meet with Donald Trump about finding a reasonable price for building a new casion [casino] in New York's financial district.

A Dominican woman in the same class wrote about what she would be doing in 20 years, when she was in her mid-30s:

> In the year 2,010 I think I will be either working still as a family lawyer or if not as a judge for the family court. After spending a hard day at my job, I would come home to cook for my husband and my two kids. Get my children's clothes ready for school tomorrow, take them a bath and get them ready for bed. So that I could leave them with there father while I went to a lawyer's get-together meeting in the night. I would leave my two floor house and go into my car and leave to the meeting, come back late, to find my husband and kids sleeping. Get into bed and await the new day to come.

A Latino man produced a passage that I love and continue to wonder about, since he is entirely clever enough to have written this as a spoof:

> When I wake up I kiss my wife put on my uniform. I think to myself I'm so important to so many people their world can't work without me. I take the plymouth to my job and then there it's my bus M104. I get in and go on my route and say Hello to everybody who get on and then move on Because I'm a Bus Driver. I feel so

proud of myself because this what I wanted to be nearly all my life
I admired bus drivers because they are so important to society and
the environment because they drive the vehicles that prevent
people to use their car and pollute the air with carbon monoxide.

When I first read them, these writings filled me with a terrible sense
of foreboding. How could I claim that this was college-level work? Was
this college work? What I've come to understand is that that is not the
right question. What I needed to learn that semester was how to be in the
room with these specific kids, instead of just sitting back, passing judgment
on their papers. I had to help them break into the peculiar combination of
wildly inflated, popular culture ambitions and disappointed fatalism they
felt, and give some reality to the role that school could play (including
grammar and spelling).

I really couldn't hear their voices accurately at first. The young man
who plans to work with Donald Trump turned out to be a fragile, marginal student in every respect; the woman who plans to be a lawyer deserves every chance to do just that; while the bus-driver-to-be, despite his
punctuation, is a splendid thinker. Was my "college course" supposed to
be equally useful to each of them? Which of the three might attend a liberal arts college? Could all of them?

There were academically strong, skillful students in the group as well,
but they didn't pose such hard questions for me. I realized pretty early on
that what I was hearing from the "underprepared" students in the class
was not remotely a lack of intelligence. One of my favorites was a Puerto
Rican man named Oscar. Oscar barely spoke in class. Each time he did,
however, I glimpsed a theoretically powerful mind and sensed how much
the material engaged him, even though he didn't yet know that about
himself. After 5 or 6 weeks I asked the class how they felt about the analytic papers they'd just written (on Skinner and Dewey) and what the most
pressing question they had on their minds was after finishing the papers.
Oscar stared out the window while the others wrote, making me think he
wouldn't do it. Then finally he scribbled for a few minutes.

What was hard (about writing this paper) was that I Needed to Get
down how to say what Actually was their feeling, B.F. Skinner and
John Dewey. Something I would like to know is How are these
people like Skinner, Dewey, Jules Henry. Are they Rich are they
poor. Is this all they do for a living. Is this their real job?

Despite the obvious errors, Oscar was raising serious questions about
thinking and how you "get it down," about socioeconomic class and pro-

fessionalism and, I venture to say, his own ambitions, since this is a young man whose intellectual gifts run so strongly to theory that he might actually want to write books for his "real job."

Just as Oscar made me recognize that the formation of serious intellectual questions could look radically different in an untracked class, Tamara and Jewel illustrated the range of interpretations of a text, another fundamental college skill. The class had read a book called *Crossing the Line* (Finnegan, 1986) about a White North American man's experiences teaching in a so-called colored secondary school in South Africa under apartheid. Tamara developed an astute analysis of the system Finnegan describes:

> Under a racial discrimination government such as Apartheid, its the governments goal to oppress and deprive blacks of an education. What is taught in there classes is exactly what the government wants them to know. For example female blacks are required to take a gardening class and the males must take a mining skills class. This implys that this is all the government will allow blacks to become.

Jewel wrote, in response to the same book:

> I don't feel that I am going through a great deal of oppression from my school system as an individual. In the passed their have been tests that could detain me. Now there are many programs that can assist one to get a high score. All one needs is self-confidence. There were programs that abled minority students to get scholarships because of their low income. This program is being terminated because it is only open to certain ethnic groups as blacks and latinos. This may be a form of oppression but it has not affected me yet but hopefully this will change.

Jewel was struggling, I think, with what education claims to be and what it has been for her, living not in South Africa but in New York City. The excerpt is confusing, but so are the messages that she has been given about education. Rather than say that Tamara "got" Finnegan's argument and Jewel didn't, I had to be able to "hear" Jewel's thinking.

My point is not that I have never seen this array of analytic or writing skills in a college class. I have, although I felt overwhelmed by my inexperience as a teacher of skills. Many of the CPESS students were strong thinkers; Tamara could have joined a 1st-year seminar that 1st week. But that was because she spoke in a voice that I knew how to hear. Other kids' voices, from Oscar's to Jewel's, were gradually instructing me in how to listen to an untracked, thoroughly heterogeneous class. I had to figure out and respond to what each student meant, insist on the skills needed to express that meaning well, and honor an ever more complex job: teaching the skills the kids needed rather than evaluating them on the basis of who had walked in the door with certain academic tools in hand.

Even as I acknowledged how much I had to learn, I still hadn't taken the measure of how much the CPESS kids' experiences in my class—or what happens to high school students whenever they find themselves in college classrooms—could have to do with their futures. If I'd been faced in an "ordinary" college class with the spectrum of competence and fluency I encountered in the CPESS class, I probably would have decided to teach to some "high-middle" group, assuming that everyone else would scramble along—or not. This decision would have determined whom I would "hear" and whom I wouldn't; I might have sent the individuals who seemed over their heads to get extra (remedial) help. Or I might have met with them outside class, assuming with an arrogance not uncommon in the university that I could make a difference.

Most important, I would have called on the unspoken (often unconscious) privilege that allows a college teacher to say that it is the student's fault, the bus driver's, or Jewel's, if he or she is having trouble, or failing. When students don't do well, college professors tend to blame it on the kids' individual limitations, or on the characteristics of some group the student belongs to, a language group or a socioeconomic or racial group. As Mike Rose (1989) says, "We seem to have a need as a society to explain poor performance by reaching deep into the basic stuff of those designated as other" (p. 222). More sophisticated people evade these prejudices by blaming the students' prior schooling, usually labeled and dismissed (like the kids) as "urban" (signifying poor and of color).

College faculty scarcely have to lift a finger when we find ourselves confronted with students who seem academically "other." The university tracks these young people into tutoring, skills classes, and the like so efficiently that we don't even hear them leaving. Their voices just disappear. High attrition rates for underprepared students, often students of color, disguise terrible injuries to individuals, since students blame themselves, not the institutions or their teachers, for their academic failures. Nobody dreams of holding the instructors accountable, much less blaming us, when a student fails.

We professors do, however, give the grades and determine who succeeds in our courses. We decide whom to listen to. It is racist and damaging, almost beyond words, to welcome "diverse" young people, some of whom are underprepared, onto our campuses only to tell them we're sorry, but they're not ready, or simply can't do whatever it is we're doing. As Lisa Delpit (1995) asserts:

> We cannot justifiably enlist exclusionary standards where the reason this student lacked the skills demanded was poor teaching at best and institutionalized racism at worst. . . . The answer is to accept students but also to take responsibility to teach them. (p. 38)

Delpit's "answer" is the same one that CPESS and other pioneering high schools offer when they insist that a democratic school community must be untracked. Schooling is itself a formidable sorting process in American culture, virtually independent of the countless differences that children bring with them when they start school. The small high schools at the forefront of school reform are challenging the most venerated sorting systems—for example, standardized testing—at the same time as they invent good teaching practice for heterogeneous classrooms.

Among the many accomplishments these schools have to be proud of is their graduation record: More students are progressing further than anyone would have dreamed possible had the same young people attended huge, factory-model high schools. Beginning with the first graduating class in 1989, more than 90% of the graduates from CPESS have gone on to college (Darling-Hammond, Ancess, & Falk, 1995). This is a radical experiment; college teachers can't afford just to sit back and watch what happens.

I am now convinced that any one of these kids (Oscar, or Jewel, or the girl who wants to be a judge) might discover what he or she loves and wants to study in college, in my classroom. But that won't happen unless I see it as my job to teach the rules of the academic game (what Delpit calls the culture of power) to students for whom it is all new, often frightening and overwhelming. For those of us who are ourselves middle- or upper-middle-class professional people, usually White, this is a big step. To adopt this stance requires the suspension of long-held preconceptions about the relation between academic abilities, (lions, tigers, and giraffes), or "merit," and an individual's success and achievements in college and in life after school.

One of my students, a Chinese woman who had lived in the United States for 4 or 5 years, a senior and an excellent student, once told me:

> I will be graduating from Cornell in business. Then I received masters degree in business administration or management. Worked very hard in my company and was noticed by the president and he then gave me a promotion. I don't think this day in 2010 will exist

because it's too perfect. I don't think I'll have this luck, but this has always been my dream.

As this and the other student voices I have quoted indicate, I've often asked the high school students how they see their futures, searching for their plans and dreams and hopes so that I (and they) might hang the intellectual habits they need on those hooks. I wanted the CPESS kids to feel the joy of using their minds well, the comfort of reading during a painful time in their lives, the thrill of grasping something really difficult. But I also wanted their academic work to connect to their own goals for their educations.

Perhaps the most important lesson I've learned from the high school students has two parts: first, the level of academic skills or "preparedness" (which does, often, correlate with socioeconomic class) is the most telling background information to have when kids make the transition from public high school into liberal arts colleges; and, second, we can't know what "underprepared" individuals will be able to do unless and until we who are their teachers announce that we will help them make the university world their own.

College teachers must not allow the needs and concerns of underprepared students to remain marginal to the intellectual life (or other resources) of our institutions. Nor can we ignore our responsibilities as teachers of increasingly heterogeneous groups of students. This is no small charge. Even in our own classes it is almost unbelievably easy to allow tracking to slide into place, to enact our fatalistic, sometimes unwitting roles in policing it, and, given that many of the students in question are people of color, to protect the university culture for a privileged White elite.

The idea of democratic educational opportunity is one many of us defend as vital to public education in this country, even as we research its failures and critique it as ideology. We may believe, for instance, that everyone should have the "opportunity" to have a college education. But who among university professors has ever dreamed that this could be a reality?

The absence of tracking represented in my CPESS course is virtually unthinkable in a college setting because the admissions hurdles people must jump over to get there, and the internal structures they encounter when they arrive, are their own firmly entrenched system of tracking. Yet, whatever the level or kind of institution, relatively more students are showing up in our classes who are relatively underprepared. Their presence signals an enormous opening, a historic moment in which we might make a difference in the lives of these courageous young people. Who among us knows how to teach effectively the range of students graduating from

CPESS? Who will help them get the tools they need, in order to have the futures this wonderful high school has encouraged them to plan for?

Listen to one last student voice:

> In the year 2002 I will have graduated from college and going to veterinarian school. Today I am to take some x-rays of a brown German short hair pointers neck because he had slipped a disk in the upper part of his neck. I will have to keep the dog for four days to continue more tests for lime disease and etc. I will have to prescribe a pain reliever for the dog. I'll have at least 15 patients a day and I leave my job at five o'clock. I drive home to the Village, stop at pizza hut and order a half a pie. I get home and eat, get undressed, take a warm bath and then go to bed. That's how each day of my life goes. Sometimes its even more distressful. My culture will always be an important part of my life, no matter what I do. I will be a positive role model for young latino people.

This is the voice of a 16-year-old Puerto Rican woman, a shy, almost silent, seemingly powerless female, a student you could easily miss. I almost missed her in my class. Yet what an impressive, potentially powerful vision she has of herself in the future. It is I who must challenge my assumptions about her, if I am to help her become that powerful adult.

This young woman who wants to be a vet knows that her school and her teachers are behind her, and Oscar knows that, even though he wonders whether writing books is a "real job." Now, college teachers must learn to hear these students' voices too. None of us can know what life will bring these kids; we can't conceivably know where they will be in 10 or 20 years, in the sense that we might think we "know" for members of our families, or for the kinds of students who have traditionally attended selective private colleges. What we can know is what happens to them while they are our students—whether we help them acquire confidence and skills or frighten or discourage them, whether we fight for them when they have trouble or shrug and turn away, unable to hear them because they are "underprepared."

The reason that the absence of tracking is such a deeply radical idea, if I had to pick just one, is that it creates a community of learners in which every single young person can say, "I plan to be somebody."

REFERENCES

Darling-Hammond, L., Ancess, J., & Falk, B. (1995). *Authentic assessment in action: Studies of schools and students at work.* New York: Teachers College Press.

Delpit, L. (1995). *Other people's children: Cultural conflict in the classroom.* New York: The New Press.

Finnegan, W. (1986). *Crossing the line: A year in the land of apartheid.* New York: Harper and Row.

Rose, M. (1989). *Lives on the boundary: The struggles and achievements of America's underprepared.* New York: The Free Press.

CHAPTER 15

After Katrina: Tales from a Chartered School Classroom

Nicole Polier

IN THE YEARS before Hurricane Katrina, public education in New Orleans was financially bankrupt and beset with administrative and accounting problems widely characterized as corruption. Before landfall leveled the system completely, the Louisiana State Superintendent of Schools hired Alvarez and Marsal, a corporate firm from New York City specializing in what it calls "turnaround management and corporate advisory services," to run New Orleans public schools, giving them a mandate to recommend changes directly to the state superintendent.[1] In late 2006, as state officials took over 107 of 128 New Orleans public schools ("School System May Limit Admissions," 2006), the state board of education had already devised what one board member calls a "state school accountability model" and began to rank schools internally.

Then came the storm.

Katrina has been described by the state superintendent of schools as something of a "cloud with a silver lining" that has made the reinvention of public education both politically possible and expedient. In the immediate aftermath of Katrina the state determined that those few schools to reopen in New Orleans would do so as chartered schools. In November 2005, for instance, the legislature voted to place 102 public schools considered "low performing" in a state-run "recovery district," leaving only 15 under district control. Of those 15, 8 have already become chartered schools, while 4 were too damaged to reopen this school year ("Two More Schools Opening Next Month," 2006). The superintendent of schools hopes to attract private funding for chartered schools from the likes of such national notables as KIPP (Knowledge Is Power Program) and the Bill and Melinda Gates Foundation.

Meanwhile, the language of academic standards, statewide test scores, discipline, individual initiative, and mental ownership has been inserted into the political discourse on public education at every level, as has the promise of private management as a panacea for public rot.

Early in 2006, all teachers laid off after Katrina who had not been re-hired were permitted to reapply for teaching positions as employees-at-will. Of 500 who reapplied, 250 were eliminated at once for failing to satisfactorily answer a question about why they chose teaching as a livelihood. The re-maining applicants were subjected to a written test consisting of math questions reportedly at eighth-grade level, and a short essay on "why I chose a career in teaching," which was corrected for spelling and grammar. Of these 250, 50 flunked, and follow-up interviews reduced the remaining applicants to a pool of 100. ("Five Charters in Algiers Set to Open Today," 2005).

The public spectacle of testing the teachers and publicizing their poor grades was touted by critics to show the failure of the old system and the straitjacket of organized labor, even under a weak union. As one news story reported, "Hiring based on merit is a marked change from rules that have bound the New Orleans public school district under its teachers' union contract" ("Five Charters in Algiers Set to Open Today," 2005).

While "rampant inefficiencies" of the old system have been replaced, greater power has been put in the hands of individual principals, who may—though it's still unclear—have more power to control budgets and design curriculums. Principals also have the autonomy to hire and fire teachers—who, under the charter system, lack even the formerly weak protection of the teachers' union—at the end of the coming school year.

Not surprisingly, the results of these changes have been internally uneven and are likely to heighten inequalities of class and color within the blighted city. As this goes to press, New Orleans public school officials are debating selective admissions requirements for four schools, and this number may increase. While these four schools were selective before the storm, given the limited number of schools open in the aftermath of Katrina, admissions criteria will widen the gap between haves and have-nots ("School System May Limit Admissions," 2006), as kids who don't make the cut are consigned to recovery districts—where the "lowest per-forming" schools were taken over by the state. As the admissions game creates segregation, schools that don't play the game will become what one board member describes as a "dumping ground" ("School System May Limit Admissions," 2006).

Chris Mayfield, a high school English teacher in New Orleans before and after Katrina, reflected on the fallout from a personal and practical standpoint. At the time we met in January 2006, Mayfield, who has been without an apartment since the hurricane and is camping out at the home of a colleague, sat grading a large stack of student papers on a Saturday afternoon in a café in the Algiers school district. These are her thoughts on current inequalities within the New Orleans chartered school system:

> I first came to New Orleans in 1986, and I've been teaching in the public schools in New Orleans for 12 years. . . . I was at Lusher School for 5 years, where I was an eighth-grade language arts instructor. After that I spent a 1-year sabbatical in India. I was at Lusher until last year.
>
> At the beginning of this year [fall 2005], I moved to become a teacher of remedial reading at the Signature Center. There, I was teaching Title I with kids below grade level in reading, primarily 10th graders. In the days leading up to landfall I was screening and scheduling students and listening to them read. I had screened some 30 students and had lots more to go.
>
> They are fabulous kids even though they have reading problems. I asked all my students who were unable to read—and I mean really unable to read, simple words—if they would be willing to forego an elective for additional reading instruction. Every student said absolutely yes, they would gladly give up an elective to take remedial reading. I left school with the student folders under my arm, and on Sunday I left town with these same folders, expecting to return to school and the students shortly.
>
> After Katrina, the Signature School was totally ruined. When I returned to the school in January—somebody had a key, and we were able to enter the building—people had been living on the second floor in my classroom. There was human shit all over the floor, and empty soup cans. But none of the Dell computers in the classroom had been so much as touched.
>
> I spent the months after Katrina in North Carolina, where I have family, returning on January 6. I talked to someone at Walker about a job and I came back with the assurance that a job would be waiting for me, which it was. I am now teaching 10th and 12th graders at Walker. Some kids in my classes are reading well below grade level and can't write; others are emotionally disturbed; any number of students work nights, and some are on their own without parents around. I've got one student working the night shift at Rally's, and even though I don't let students sleep in my classroom, for the life of me I can't wake her up. Another student tells me she has fluid in her lungs; she's living alone, and I suggested she get medical care. "Ms. Mayfield," she asked me, "now, who's going to take me to see a doctor?"

I . . . complained to Alvarez and Marsal that my principal had made me a sub, and was told . . . that the principal has no authority over employment determinations like whether an English teacher can be classified as a substitute and paid a pittance. I said, "I guess this is why we had union contracts," and I was told by them, quote unquote, "We don't want anything to do with the unions because we want teachers who are there for the kids."

Under the charter school system we no longer have a union contract. Under the union contract we would have 10 minutes of "duty" in the morning and 10 in the afternoon, or maybe we'd have lunch duty, and in any event there was some duty each day, and generally your lunch was your own time. Now, we have hours of duty. At Walker, we have some 2 hours of duty each day; the day starts at 8:00 a.m. and ends at 4:00, and there's talk that we may be forced to come in to school on Saturdays. I get to work at 7:00. Sunday is spent grading student work and class planning. As for faculty meetings, which were once regulated by contract, they are no longer, and we can have meetings whenever.

They think that, to have good schools they just open up a vein and drain your blood directly into your students. That's the way it is.

It's true that academically bankrupt schools certainly existed; but the other side of that story is that Tony Amato, the former school superintendent, really turned things around. In retrospect, his tenure was the golden age. Mr. Amato required an uninterrupted literacy block for every student and he trained the teachers, all of us, in teaching literacy. I learned a lot from Mr. Amato. And as a result of his work, test scores went way up. True, there may have been some financial mismanagement under Mr. Amato, but he did great, great work. He was serious about teacher training and professional development. It was a real mistake to have gotten rid of Mr. Amato.

But the power structure in this town does not want well-educated kids. . . . The power structure, which by the way is not all White but is Black and White, wants to produce people who can work in the service sector, and nothing more. As for the transition to charter schools, the consensus among rank-and-file union members is that they've wanted to go exclusively charter for quite some time, and Katrina was their chance. Charter schools are not innately odious. Think of Deborah Meier, who started some charter schools in Harlem; small can be effective, and I am certainly not opposed to alternative models. But the bottom line is that they should not be exclusive, and the problem with charter schools is that without open enrollment they are inherently inequitable.

O. Perry Walker is the ghetto school in this hierarchy, and Karr is the upper echelon. Harte is getting there. I'm told there are staffing differences. I have 42 students, though I understand Walker is about to hire another English teacher, which will lighten my load.

Autonomy? There is no autonomy. The school has no budget. Period. No supplies; not so much as a paper clip. There are kids who cannot read, and no plan for them. I have students in the 10th grade who cannot read the word *heartbeat*.

I've got the 10th graders writing their memoirs; they say they can keep on writing, since there's so much to say. And I have them reading from "The Neighborhood Story Project," which came out shortly before Katrina and which describes neighborhoods which are no more. There are huge attendance and class-cutting problems these days, which are not being addressed in any systematic way whatsoever. Ms. Laurie has a mandatory morning assembly for teachers and students, which may sound like a good idea, but she can't be heard, even though she yells, and so students talk through assembly and then Ms. Laurie screams at the teachers to make the students be quiet.[2]

During the day she yells orders over the school PA loud-speaker. Lunch goes on for way too long, and then she sends a security guard to announce lunch is over and sweep the hallways to make sure the students are in class. All of this is happening quite suddenly as Ms. Laurie is shouting into the PA: "Students, get to your classrooms: 10, 9, 8, 7, 6, 5, 4, 3, 2, 1! Teachers, lock your doors. Do not allow students to enter!" But we have no locks on our doors. And get this, the principal of my school, who praises the students on one hand, tells them that if they don't conform to the rules, they can leave, and that for their spot there are two to three students who would gladly take their place. "And you will have no place to go!" she tells them. . . . She's started expelling students and telling them not to return to school without a parent. This is done ad hoc, with no disciplinary procedures, no hearing office as there used to be, no student advocate as there used to be, and it seems rather capricious. Every day there is a new "Do Not Admit" list, and students are being put onto the street.

Meanwhile, there is a waiting list of 80 students who want to get into Walker High and have to wait. What sense is that? This is supposed to be a public school, and students are being turned away to wait on the street.

We don't have appropriate books for teaching English; Ms. Laurie has provided us with some books from the middle school, but they're not developmentally at age level and I can't use them. I have only textbooks and mimeographs.

It saddens me so. Here's this entity that we love so much—New Orleans—but I don't see a positive outcome from the Katrina catastrophe. It's like loving someone with a terminal illness.

The feeling I get from the charter school movement in Algiers is that there are no rules; there are no checks and balances; there is no hearing office; no teacher's union; we don't even know how we're supposed to be grading students. The treatment of students by the administration is totally ad hoc, and this is not changing. Yes, it's true what I said earlier, that the schools within the parish had been balkanized, and within them, the classrooms have been balkanized. You just go into your classroom and hope for the best.

NOTES

Thanks to Jed Horne of the New Orleans *Times-Picayune*, Chris Mayfield, Richard Ohmann, and Saul Slapikoff for their thoughtful comments on an earlier draft. This discussion is based on interviews in fall 2005 and winter 2006 with New Orleans school board members, the state superintendent of schools, teachers, parents, and community activists.

1. Alvarez and Marsal had its contract extended in March 2006, though its duties are to be slowly turned over to full-time charter association staff members ("Charter Schools Extend Contracts," 2006).

2. Mayfield recently told me that morning meeting at O. Perry Walker is less harrowing than it was 6 months ago.

REFERENCES

Five charters in Algiers set to open today. (2005, December 14). *Times-Picayune.*
School system may limit admissions. (2006, May 18). *Times-Picayune.*
Two more schools opening next month. (2006, January 29). *Times-Picayune.*

Paulo Freire: On Hope

Kathleen Weiler

IN ONE OF his last books, Paulo Freire (1998a) tells this story:

> Once, in a TV report about landless rural workers in the interior of Sao Paulo, the reporter asked a country adolescent, "Do you usually dream?" "No, I only have nightmares," he replied. What was fundamental in his answer was his fatalist, immobilist understanding. The bitterness of that adolescent's existence was so profound that his presence in the world had become a nightmare, an experience in which it was impossible to dream. (p. 45)

For hundreds of millions of people, the condition of their lives is such that, like this Brazilian teenager, they may view their existence as a living nightmare, with no possibility of a dream. This fatalism and rejection of hope reflects a material reality of poverty and exploitation that those of us in the privileged West or the privileged elites throughout the world—the First World in the Third World, to paraphrase Freire—can barely imagine. But those of us who are privileged have our own fatalisms, grounded in our sense of powerlessness, of being out of control, of living in the heart of what seems increasingly a brutal and militarized empire. What hope do we have of countering and resisting the power of the amoral and profoundly antidemocratic elites who control our government and our lives and who shape the parameters of possibility for the lives of all the people of the earth?

Consider some other teenagers, these described by Arundhati Roy (2003) in a column published during the U.S. invasion of Iraq:

> On the steel torsos of their missiles, adolescent American soldiers scrawl colorful messages in childish handwriting: For Saddam, from the Fat Boy Posse. A building goes down. A marketplace. A home. A girl who loves a boy. A child who only ever wanted to play with his brother's marbles. On March 21, the day after American and British troops began their illegal in-

vasion and occupation of Iraq, an "embedded" CNN correspondent interviewed an American soldier. "I wanna get in there and get my nose dirty,"
Private AJ said. "I wanna take revenge for 9/11." To be fair to the correspondent . . . he did sort of weakly suggest that so far there was no real evidence
that linked the Iraqi government to the September 11 attacks. . . . "Yeah,
well that stuff's way over my head," [Private AJ] replied. (p. 2)

This teenager does not awake with nightmares (or at least not that
we know) but he does not have a dream of hope either. Instead, state-
sponsored ignorance leaves teenaged soldiers like this immersed in a day-
dream of false hopes of revenge, marked by their dismissal of the possibility
of a critical reading of the world, of the stuff that's "way over [their] heads."
In his extraordinary speech, "We Stand Passively Mute," delivered on the
floor of the U.S. Senate in early February 2003, Senator Robert Byrd said,
"To engage in war is always to pick a wild card. And war must always be
a last resort, not a first choice. I truly must question the judgment of any
President who can say that a massive unprovoked military attack on a
nation which is over 50% children is 'in the highest moral traditions of
our country.'" "In our actions and words," said Byrd, "we are truly 'sleepwalking through history.'"

Nightmares, fantasies, sleepwalking. Where can we look for a positive dream of a more just world? Where is that source of hope? In her
discussion of the explosion of anti-American feeling throughout the world,
Arundhati Roy cautions against conflating a government and its people.
She notes the extraordinary demonstrations by Americans against the
actions of our government. These echo the antiwar demonstrations
throughout the world. Here in the United States and in many other countries, the peace movements are led by groups also active in anti–corporate
globalization movements and movements for more specific issues such as
trafficking in women, the destruction of the environment, the massive
human costs of such agreements as NAFTA and GATT on specific communities. These global movements are activated by a hope that a more
just world can come into being. For the past 3 decades, teachers, literacy
workers, and those who believe in the possibility of critical teaching and
learning have found a similar source of hope in the work of Paulo Freire.
What can Paulo Freire contribute to our understanding of the possibilities
of hope in this extreme historical moment?

Since the publication of *Pedagogy of the Oppressed* more than 30 years
ago, Paulo Freire has been an inspiration to progressive educators seeking
ways to use education to build more just societies in settings throughout
the world. Freire's compassion and eloquence speak powerfully to all those
seeking social justice and have led many educators to claim Freire as their

own. Freire stood firmly with the oppressed, and the consistency of his vision has made him a symbol of resistance to oppression. To the very end of his life, Freire continued to condemn forces of exploitation and dehumanization. While acknowledging his limitations, I believe we can look to Freire as an example of what it means to be an engaged educator seeking peace and justice in a militarized and deeply unjust world.

A large part of Freire's appeal lies in his eloquence and steadfast denunciation of injustice. But another is the simplicity of the initial vision of the world that he expressed in *Pedagogy of the Oppressed*: There are two positions, oppressor and oppressed; both are examples of dehumanization, but only the oppressed can lead the struggle for true humanization, because they are the ones who truly understand "the terrible significance of an oppressive society" (1998b, p. 27). For Freire in *Pedagogy of the Oppressed*, true humanization is marked by freedom, autonomy, and responsibility. Following existentialist thinkers like Erich Fromm, Freire sees freedom as "the indispensable condition for the quest for human completion" (p. 29). If Freire had remained at this level of idealism, he would have remained an academic philosopher framing the world in binary abstractions. It is Freire's next step that makes his work so influential.

For Freire, the oppressed must see that the limitations of their freedom are not inevitable, but are the result of actions taken to construct and maintain an unjust world. But this perception of an unjust world that is not fated, but that has come about because of historical struggle, is also not enough. It must lead to action, to praxis, the struggle to transform that violent world.

For Freire violence is a key concept. For him, violence refers not only to the kind of violence with which we now are all too familiar—the missiles, bombs, deaths and maiming of civilians and teenaged soldiers—but also the violence of the status quo, of an unjust society that distorts and limits the possibility of full humanity to masses of people—people who are not even seen as human by those in power. For the oppressors, "any situation other than their former seems to them like oppression" (1998b, p. 39). They are accustomed to seeing only themselves as humans; others are simply things, to be exploited or possessed. As Freire put it:

> In their unrestrained eagerness to possess, the oppressors develop the conviction that it is possible for them to transform everything into objects of their purchasing power; hence their strictly materialistic concept of existence. Money is the measure of all things, and profit the primary goal. For the oppressors, what is worthwhile is to have more—always more—even at the cost of the oppressed having less or having nothing. For them, to be is to have. (p. 40)

Through their control of the state and the media, through the sheer magnitude of their wealth and willingness to use violence to maintain it, elites have been able to define and control the world. Their vision comes to permeate the consciousness of all. This is why Freire insists that action alone will not suffice. Until the oppressed develop new conceptions of what humane relationships can be, they will be faced by the constant danger that they will simply replicate the world they are seeking to transform. Thus praxis, the dialectic of reflection and action, is the source of hope, grounded in Freire's (1998b) unswerving conviction of the human capacity for love and thirst for justice.

> Nor yet can dialogue exist without hope. Hope is rooted in men's incompletion, from which they move out in constant search—a search which can be carried out only in communion with others. Hopelessness is a form of silence, of denying the world and fleeing from it. (p. 73)

The hope that marks *Pedagogy of the Oppressed* reflects the moment of revolution and sense of radical possibility of the late 1960s. This confidence and certainty can be seen in the binary quality of Freire's thinking, his comfort with the position of the leader who calls for revolutionary action, his failure to address the complexity of overlapping and contradictory positions in which the positions of oppressor and oppressed are shifting and ambiguous. For Freire, as for other left critics of this period, this revolutionary hero is imagined as male and as existing solely in the public world, a vision that discounts and yet at the same time rests on the world of personal relationships or of everyday life—the world of women.[1] Freire's work has been challenged by feminists and postmodernists, who call into question his unexamined assumption of male privilege and his modernist faith in rationality and historical metanarratives.

In his later work, Freire moved to a more nuanced discussion of hope that acknowledged the complexity of conflicting discourses and positions. But despite his recognition of the challenges raised by feminism and postmodernism, Freire never abandoned his commitment to hope. This insistence is in part strategic. For him, those who reject hope, who discount human agency and the possibility of a better world as utopian idealism are themselves actively contributing to an oppressive world by encouraging fatalism. For Freire, fatalism was a quality expressed not only by the poor and oppressed who could not imagine a different world, but also by those intellectuals who reject any possibility of action in the world because it will always be compromised by uncertainty, never "true." Or by those who are overwhelmed by the tactics of economic "shock and awe," by the alliance of global corporations who seek to strip the world of its resources and the militarized state that polices the policies that allow that devastation. In his later work, Freire spoke of the destruction caused by this form of economic globalization. But he refused to abandon hope of resistance to these seemingly inexorable forces.

For Freire, hope is central for strategic progressive change. It is not enough in itself, but without hope, a vision of a better future, a dream of possibility, we sink into immobility and despair. Freire is well aware of the balance between utopian hope and concrete analysis. As he puts it in *Pedagogy of Hope*: "I do not mean that, because I am hopeful, I attribute to this hope of mine the power to transform reality all by itself, so that I set out for the fray without taking account of concrete, material data, declaring, 'My hope is enough!'" (1994, p. 8). Freire points out that naive hope without analysis is a recipe for disillusion and cynical pessimism. Instead he calls for "critical hope," a hope grounded in careful analysis and understanding of an historical situation and a move to action. Critical hope is grounded in an understanding of the dialectical relationship of critical understanding and material conditions. It understands the future not as simply a repetition of today or as the inevitable march of progress. We can have hope about the future not because progress is inevitable or because God is on our side or because we believe it is our destiny to control the world, but because the future will be made through the struggles of human beings. Only in that struggle will our vision for a more just society be possible:

> In the dialectical perception, the future of which we dream is not inexorable. We have to make it, produce it, else it will not come in the form that we would more or less wish it to. True, of course, we have to make it not arbitrarily, but with the materials, with the concrete reality, of which we dispose, and more as a project, a dream, for which we struggle. (1994, p. 101)

Freire's distinction between utopian hope and critical hope is similar to Berenice Fisher's contrast between what she calls "promissory hope" and "cautionary hope." By "promissory hope" she is referring to the belief—particularly prevalent in the revolutionary moment of the late 1960s—that social movements would lead to, in Fisher's words, "a near-perfect social world" (2001, p. 192). She contrasts that to the "cautionary hope" that has developed in response to the growth of neoliberalism, the collapse of the Soviet Union, the seeming triumph of corporate globalization. "Cautionary hope," similar to Foucault's emphasis on micro power and local sites of resistance, focuses on the need for and importance of local struggles. It does not assume that a just and peaceful future is either inevitable or impossible, but asserts the importance of maintaining our values and goals and fighting for them in whatever setting we find ourselves. In her discussion of the complexities of this relationship of global and local hopes based on her own teaching, Fisher notes that if a sense of larger possibility is lost, students' "small hopes shrivel, no longer so secure" (2001, p. 193). But when the local is shown to be flawed, a belief in the possibility of large-scale progressive change can also be threatened. For example, when students of color motivated to build a more just society experience racism from those they have taken to be their allies, they may lose hope that a broad movement for change is feasible. The same is true for women if they meet sexism and condescension from men they have seen as gender allies.

In her discussion of these complex manifestations of hope, Fisher speaks of "grounded hope," a hope that emerges from her appreciation of the possibilities of human growth and change and her sense of the richness of classroom exchanges in her own teaching. As she puts it, "This sense of promise is neither great nor small, but grounded in the continued interactions among class members, myself, and the world" (2001, p. 194). This means creating opportunities for dialogue and, most important, respect for students' voices, and an understanding that they can create spaces for progressive change that she as a teacher might never have imagined. Speaking of feminist teachers, Fisher writes that they "cannot be certain which forms of action will be most effective in achieving gender and other kinds of social justice" (p. 196). These forms of action will emerge from the life circumstances and perceptions of students in reference to their own local struggles. What Fisher offers is her hope and belief in the possibility of progressive change, her respect for students as meaning-making human beings, and her sense that the future is not inevitable, but will be made by human actions in the world.

Berenice Fisher's discussion of the grounds for hope in her students supports Freire's assertion that history is the result of human choices and not a determined or fated narrative in which we as human beings are simply spectators. As Freire argues in a late essay:

> I insist that history is possibility and not determinism. We are conditioned beings but not determined beings. It is impossible to understand history as possibility if we do not recognize human beings as beings who make free decisions. Without this form of exercise it is not worth speaking about ethics. (1998a, p. 37)

This understanding of history as possibility and the result of human actions means there is always the possibility of change. We do not live at the end of history; quite the contrary, as the events of the past decade have reminded us so forcefully, we live in the midst of a bewildering and almost unfathomable period of rapid historical change. Asserting hope or claiming the possibility of a better world does not automatically bring that better world into being. Freire continued to insist on the dialectic of analysis and action, of praxis, until the end of his life. As he wrote of liberation:

> Hope of liberation does not mean liberation already. It is necessary to fight for it, within historically favorable conditions. If they do not exist, we must hopefully labor to create them. Liberation is a possibility, not fate nor destiny nor burden. In this context, one can realize the importance of education for decision, for rupture, for choice, for ethics at last. (1998a, p. 44)

Freire never loses sight of this central claim: that the world we live in is the result of human action, that the future will be made by human beings, that history is not static and unchanging, that the oppressive reality we see around us can be transformed.

These themes of oppression, history, and the need for hope in the present moment, which for me as an American is a moment of shame and despair, were strikingly raised by Ariel Dorfman (2004) in his poem "An Open Letter to America," written after the September 11 attacks. I end with a section from that poem, which speaks to the stubborn hope that a more just world is possible:

> My hope for America: empathy,
> compassion, the capacity to
> imagine that you are not unique.
> Yes, America, if this dreadful destruction were only to teach
> you that your citizens and your
> dead are not the only ones who
> matter on this planet,
> if that experience were to lead
> you to wage a resolute war on the
> multiple terrors
> that haunt our already
> murderous new century.
> An awakening, America.
> Not to be. What did not happen.
> Am I wrong to believe that the
> country that gave the world jazz
> and Faulkner and Eleanor
> Roosevelt
> will be able to look at itself in the
> cracked mirror of history and
> join the rest of humanity,

not as a city on a separate hill,
but as one more city in the
shining valleys
of sorrow and uncertainty and
hope where we all dwell?

NOTE

1. Dorothy Smith (1987) has analyzed this split extensively. See also Yeatman, 1994, and Hennesey, 1993.

REFERENCES

Byrd, R. C. (2003, February 12). We stand passively mute. Speech delivered on the floor of the United States Senate. Retrieved March 8, 2008, from http://www.guardian.co.uk/world/2003/feb18/usa.iraq

Dorfman, A. (2004). An open letter to America. In A. Dorfman, *Other Septembers, many Americas: Selected provocations, 1980–2004.* New York: Seven Stories Press.

Fisher, B. (2001). *No angel in the classroom.* New York: Rowman and Littlefield.

Freire, P. (1994). *Pedagogy of hope.* New York: Continuum.

Freire, P. (1998a). *Pedagogy of the heart.* New York: Continuum.

Freire, P. (1998b). *Pedagogy of the oppressed.* New York: Continuum.

Hennesey, R. (1993). *Materialist feminism and the politics of discourse.* New York: Routledge.

Roy, A. (2003, April 2). Mesopotamia. Babylon. The Tigris and Euphrates. *The Guardian,* Comments and Features section.

Smith, D. E. (1987). *The everyday world as problematic.* Lebanon, NH: University Press of New England.

Yeatman, A. (1994). *Postmodern revisionings of the political.* New York: Routledge.

About the Editors and the Contributors

BERNADETTE ANAND, an instructor and advisor in the graduate school at Bank Street College, was the founding principal of Renaissance Middle School in Montclair, New Jersey. She has long been involved with struggles for detracking and social justice through educational excellence for all.

NANCY BARNES is a cultural anthropologist who is on the faculty at Lang College, the undergraduate college of the New School. Her ethnographic research, often done in collaboration with public school teachers, has centered on the small new high schools in New York City. She currently works with a high-school-to-college transition program and is writing a book about the pleasures of a teaching life.

LILIA I. BARTOLOMÉ is Professor in the Applied Linguistics Graduate Program at the University of Massachusetts, Boston. As a teacher educator, she pursues research interests that include the preparation of effective teachers of minority and second-language learners in multicultural contexts. In particular, Bartolomé examines teacher ideological orientations around their work with linguistic-minority students as well as their actual classroom practices with this student population. Her books are *Ideologies in Education: Unmasking the Trap of Teacher Neutrality* (in press), *The Misteaching of Academic Discourses, Immigrant Voices: In Search of Pedagogical Equity* (with Henry Trueba), and *Dancing with Bigotry: The Poisoning of Culture* (with Donaldo Macedo).

BILL BIGELOW (bbpdx@aol.com) has taught social studies in Portland, Oregon, since 1978. He is an editor of *Rethinking Schools* magazine. His most recent book is *The Line Between Us: Teaching About the Border and Mexican Immigration* (2006).

LAWRENCE BLUM is Distinguished Professor of Liberal Arts and Education, and Professor of Philosophy, at the University of Massachusetts, Boston, where he teaches moral philosophy, race studies, and multicultural education. He is the author of *"I'm Not a Racist, But . . .": The Moral Quandary of Race*, published in 2002. He can be reached at lawrence.blum@umb .edu.

JOSEPH ENTIN (Editor) teaches English and American Studies at Brooklyn College, City University of New York, and serves on the editorial board of *Radical Teacher*. He is the author of *Sensational Modernism: Experimental Fiction and Photography in Thirties America* (2007).

MARJORIE FELD is assistant professor of history at Babson College, where she teaches courses on U.S. gender, labor, and immigration history. Her biography of Lillian Wald is forthcoming from the University of North Carolina Press. She has been on the board of *Radical Teacher* since 1997.

MICHELLE FINE is Distinguished Professor of Social Psychology and Urban Education at the Graduate Center, City University of New York, and has long been involved in participatory action research with youth, critical prison studies, and urban educational reform and has (for almost as long) been awed by the incredible work of Dr. Anand and her colleagues.

After serving for 3 years as a navigator and intelligence officer in the Strategic Air Command, H. BRUCE FRANKLIN became a prominent figure in the movement against the Vietnam War. The author or editor of 19 books and more than 300 articles on culture and history, he is currently the John Cotton Dana Professor of English and American Studies at Rutgers University in Newark.

STAN KARP is an editor of *Rethinking Schools* magazine and has written widely on school reform and educational policy. His articles have appeared in *Education Week* and *Educational Leadership*, and he is a coeditor of several books, including *Rethinking Our Classrooms: Teaching for Equity and Justice*, and *Rethinking School Reform: Views from the Classroom*. For 30 years, he taught English and Journalism to high school students in Paterson, New Jersey. He is currently director of the Secondary Reform Project for New Jersey's Education Law Center.

KEVIN K. KUMASHIRO, PhD, is an associate professor of policy studies at the University of Illinois–Chicago College of Education and is the founding director of the Center for Anti-Oppressive Education. He has authored or edited several books, including the award-winning *Troubling Education: Queer Activism and Anti-oppressive Pedagogy* and, more recently, *Against Common Sense: Teaching and Learning toward Social Justice*.

Pepi Leistyna is an associate professor of applied linguistics graduate studies at the University of Massachusetts, Boston, where he coordinates the research program and teaches courses in cultural studies, media literacy, and language acquisition. He speaks internationally on issues of democracy, public education, and social justice, and his books include *Breaking Free: The Transformative Power of Critical Pedagogy, Presence of Mind: Education and the Politics of Deception, Defining and Designing Multiculturalism, Cultural Studies: From Theory to Action,* and *Corpus Analysis: Language Structure and Language Use.* He is coeditor of *Book Smarts* and is a research fellow of the Educational Policy Research Unit at Arizona State University and of the Education and Public Interest Center at the University of Colorado. His recent documentary film is called *Class Dismissed: How TV Frames the Working Class,* for which he is the 2007 recipient of the Studs Terkel Award for Media and Journalism.

Arthur MacEwan is the chair of the Department of Economics at the University of Massachusetts, Boston. His analysis of globalization and related matters is developed in *Neo-liberalism or Democracy? Economic Strategy, Markets, and Alternatives of the 21st Century.* He is a founder of *Dollars & Sense* magazine, for which he writes regularly.

Sarah Napier taught in a fifth/sixth-grade classroom at the Paideia School in Atlanta, Georgia for 2 years. She also worked on the board of the Women's Resource Center of DeKalb County and for the Georgia Abortion Rights Action League. At this writing, she was in a master's program at the Harvard Graduate School of Education and planning to continue teaching elementary school.

Bob Peterson (repmilw@aol.com) teaches fifth grade at La Escuela Fratney in Milwaukee, Wisconsin, and is an editor of *Rethinking Schools.* He and Bill Bigelow are coeditors of *Rethinking Globalization: Teaching for Justice in an Unjust World* (2002). Peterson also edited, with Eric Gutstein, *Rethinking Mathematics: Teaching Social Justice by the Numbers* (2005).

Nicole Polier is a cultural anthropologist and educator currently working as a public interest attorney in New York City.

Robert C. Rosen (Editor) teaches English at William Paterson University in New Jersey and is coeditor of *Literature and Society: An Introduction to Fiction, Poetry, Drama, Nonfiction* and of *Against the Current: Readings for Writers* and the author of *John Dos Passos: Politics and the Writer.* He is a member of the *Radical Teacher* editorial board and coeditor of *Politics of Education: Essays from Radical Teacher.*

PATTI CAPEL SWARTZ is an assistant professor of English and English coordinator for Kent State University, East Liverpool Campus. Swartz writes and presents about women's, diversity, and sexuality issues. Her work on critical pedagogy and gender has appeared in the journals *Race Gender and Class*, *Mattoid*, and *Journal of Gay, Lesbian, and Bisexual Identity*.

MARIA SWEENEY has taught Grades 2, 3, and 4 since 1986. She is currently a Reading Recovery teacher and staff developer at Travell School in Ridgewood, New Jersey.

RITA VERMA received her PhD from the University of Wisconsin–Madison in educational policy studies and curriculum and instruction. She has taught for several years in the New York public school system. Rita is currently an assistant professor in curriculum and instruction at Adelphi University in New York. She recently published a book titled *Backlash: South Asian Immigrant Voices on the Margins*.

LEONARD VOGT (Editor) is professor emeritus of English at LaGuardia Community College of the City University of New York, where for many years he was faculty co-mentor of the Straight and Gay Alliance and taught a lesbian and gay literature course; an urban study course called Art, Politics, and Protest; and composition and research in numerous liberal arts clusters centered around social history and alternative media. He was co-editor of *Politics of Education: Essays from Radical Teacher* (1990) and is a member of the *Radical Teacher* board.

KATHLEEN WEILER is professor of education at Tufts University. She has written a number of works on women and education, among them *Women Teaching for Change* (1988) and *Country Schoolwomen* (1998). Her most recent book is her edited collection *Feminist Engagements* (2001). She is a member of the *Radical Teacher* board.

Index